INSIDE THE BMW FACTORIES

BUILDING THE ULTIMATE DRIVING MACHINE

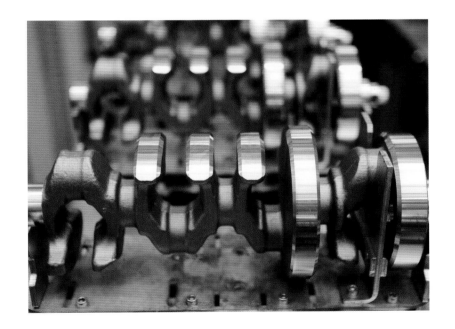

INSIDE THE
BMW FACTORIES

BUILDING THE ULTIMATE DRIVING MACHINE

GRAHAM ROBSON

motorbooks

This edition published in 2008 by Motorbooks, an imprint of MBI
Publishing Company, 400 First Avenue North, Suite 300, Minneapolis, MN
55401 USA

MBI Publishing Company titles are also available at discounts in bulk
quantity for industrial or sales-promotional use. For details write to
Special Sales Manager at MBI Publishing Company, 400 First Avenue
North, Suite 300, Minneapolis, MN 55401 USA

Library of Congress Cataloging-in-Publication Data

Robson, Graham, 1936-
Inside the BMW factories: building the ultimate driving machine / Graham
Robson.
p. cm.
Includes index.
ISBN 978-0-7603-3463-8 (hb w/ jkt)
1. BMW automobiles—History. 2. Bayerische Motoren Werke—History.
3. Automobiles—Design and construction—History. 4. Automobile
industry and trade—Germany—History. I. Title.
TL215.B25R64 2008
629.222'2—dc22
                                    2008025700
Printed in China

Designed by Sue Rose at Casebourne Rose Design Associates

CONTENTS

NINE DECADES OF EXCELLENCE

By Dr. Caroline Schulenburg and Dr. Florian Triebel

BMW GROUP CLASSIC

Even in the very early years, BMW's production process delivered both high quality and flexibility. To counterbalance the uncertainty in aircraft engine production, BMW AG began to manufacture motorcycles in 1923. This new operation was integrated into its existing production system, and highly qualified aircraft technicians swapped production duties between aero-engine and motorcycle fabrication. On account of their extremely high quality, BMW motorcycles carried high retail prices from the very beginning.

Through the purchase of the Eisenbach vehicle factory in 1928, BMW not only acquired a car production facility, but also acquired the know-how for efficient volume production. This was a completely different expertise from that necessary to manufacture the limited numbers of aircraft engines and motorcycles in the Munich factory. BMW cars immediately demonstrated the high quality that had shaped the reputation of the brand and its products in the 1920s. This image was reinforced when BMW's little car was victorious in the international alpine run of 1929.

After Hitler's rise to power in January 1933, Germany began a policy of rearmament. The importance of military equipment rose exponentially and BMW concentrated increasingly on the production of aircraft engines. The newly founded factories in Allach (near Munich) and in Dürrerhof (near Eisenach) were designed for the high quality large-scale production, in order to satisfy the Deutsche Luftwaffe's steadily growing demand for aircraft engines. This endeavour was supported by the purchase of Brandenburgische Motoren Werke GmbH in Berlin-Spandau, which took place just before the start of the Second World War.

The end of the War meant that BMW lost its factories in the Soviet occupied zone in East Germany. These plants included the production facilities at Eisenach and Dürrerhof in Thuringia, together with Zühlsdorf and Basdorf near Berlin). Production could only be continued in Munich, Allach, and Spandau. Allach was turned into a repair station for American army vehicles, and in 1948, production of machine tools began at Spandau. That only left the main factory in Munich-Milbertshofen to start the production of vehicles once again. After three years of stopgap production of cooking pots and other basic household gadgets, the manufacture of motorbikes was re-started in 1948, with the same, high pre-war quality standards. The resumption of car production in Munich, however, was a more difficult task. From 1952, the production costs of larger cars proved to be too high, and resulted in a lower quality than was expected from the brand. With the introduction of the Isetta into its production portfolio, BMW were able to achieve two simultaneous targets: to occupy the skilled workers in Allach, and to re-establish full production capacity. Just as in the 1920s, the company tried to build the production know-how of its workforce. Additionally, the workers on the Isetta production lines gained a complete experience of car production, which was essential for securing the continued existence of the company in the 1960s.

With the start of the so-called "New Class" cars in 1962, Milbertshofen faced a new production challenge. As the BMW 1500 still suffered from quality defects, a multistage system of quality inspection was introduced into the production process in 1963. The company was determined that its vehicles should meet high expectations. By 1966, the resulting success of the New Class and the 02 series models had driven the potential capacity of the plant to its limit. In 1966, BMW took the opportunity of purchasing the Hans Glas GmbH production plants in Dingolfing and Landshut. Initially, some GLAS vehicles continued to be produced. But because their design quality did not match BMW's high standards, the manufacture of GLAS vehicles was discontinued in 1968.

By the end of the 1960s, the increasing demand for BMW models meant that a radical expansion of the company's production facilities was needed. In the immediate vicinity of the former GLAS grounds in Dingolfing, a brand new BMW plant was erected in the early 1970s. It was opened in 1973, almost in the middle of the world energy crisis. But BMW ignored the slump, and began to produce 5 and 7 series cars.

The energy crisis of 1973/74 also focused attention on possible growth limits. Vehicle output went down in 1974, which convinced BMW that it must be able to accommodate fluctuations in production volume. When production was reorganized in the mid-1970s, flexibility and reliability were given equal priority. New technologies appeared on the shop floor: overhead conveyors made process sequences more efficient, and the first robot welders and freely programmable machines were installed in the body-in-white construction area. These investments in automation and new working methods meant that the workforce could be reduced in size. This both enhanced quality and reduced costs. The production structure was now more flexible and could respond easily to changes in demand. In 1975, the system had its first opportunity to prove its value: BMW was able to respond to unexpectedly strong demand from the domestic market, coupled with a drop in exports.

Since 1972, all the new model launches had gone ahead without any major hitches, but the first few weeks after the start of production will always be a critical period in a car's life-cycle. For one thing, it proves whether or not the development engineers have done their job properly. As the decade progressed, a proliferation of models meant that the company's technical systems became increasingly complex. At the end of the 1970s, the development and production divisions were brought together to find a solution to this problem. They reverted to an idea that BMW had first used in its Second World War aircraft engine production: the "pilot production line." This was a separate section of the factory in which prototype production lines were tried out under authentic conditions, so that difficulties on the assembly line could be identified before full-scale production was due to start, and a solution agreed with the development staff. Opportunities for improving the production sequence could also be explored. The new pilot scheme began in 1979 at the Munich plant.

These structural changes led to a further improvement in quality. By the end of the 1970s, assembly line work had changed to a system that employed either single or group work. This meant that each production worker had both more responsibility, and greater flexibility in his daily work. The automation of monotonous activities also resulted in a clear improvement in working conditions. The duties for the group workers on the production line were improved in the fields of logistics, maintenance, and quality standards. By the end of the 1980s, manual tasks were gradually replaced by planning and monitoring functions.

With the construction of the Regensburg plant in the first half of the 1980s, BMW realised that flexibility was not only important in production workflow, but also in the organisation of working hours. A new working "hour model," in which working hours and machine running time were disassociated from each other was achieved for the first time. Other factories followed Regensburg's lead, with gradual improvements in their own flexibility. These included the introduction of working hour "accounts," and variously structured part-time opportunities. In 1995, an agreement on new working practices came into effect, which has since become a template for many manufacturers. Group work and enhanced responsibility has also led to higher wages and a better "team spirit" among the workforce.

The increasing number of model variants and complex technical requirements has posed a permanent challenge to the company's manufacturing facilities and logistical systems. As well as increasing capacities, manufacturing processes had to be made more flexible and high quality standards maintained consistently, over long periods. At the end of the 1980s, BMW tackled these issues with a number of fundamental changes to its production structure.

Since the 1980s, the American market has gained steadily in importance for BMW. This led to the company instigating a feasibility study into the viability of an American production plant. BMW became the first European manufacturer of premium automobiles to risk such a step. The availability of suitable personnel and good infrastructural links were high on the list of priorities, so that the new plant could be integrated efficiently into BMW's production alliance. Before production started in September 1994, American employees were familiarized with BMW's methods and workflows at the Munich, Dingolfing, and Regensburg plants. This principle, tried and tested ever since production had begun back in Dingolfing in 1972, greatly contributed to a trouble-free run-up to 3 series car production, followed later by the BMW Z3.

When BMW acquired the Rover Group, the acquisition included its factories in Great Britain. Up until 1999, and with support from BMW's own production plants, intensive efforts were made to modernize the Rover Group's machines, equipment, and production methods. Even after the sale of the Rover Group in 2000, the new engine production plant in Ham's Hall, the new press shop in Swindon, and the modernized Oxford car factory (which has been used to build the MINI since 2001), remained in BMW's possession.

Towards the end of the 1990s, BMW built up two further production factories with partners in emerging markets: in cooperation with Brilliance Automotive Ltd, BMW founded a factory in north east China for the finishing of 3 and 5 series models for local sales. In BMW's home market, Germany, production in the newly-built Leipzig plant started in March 2005.

Ninety years after being established, the company now operates a flexible structure of 16 company-owned production sites for automobiles and motorcycles on four continents, as well as various other assembly facilities run in cooperation with partner-companies or importers.

TIMELINE

1898 First automobiles—Wartburgs—built at Eisenach in Germany. This brand replaced by Dixi in 1903

1913 Karl Rapp founds Rapp-Motorenwerke GMbH at 288, Schleissheimer Strasse in Munich

1916 Official date of the current BMW AG's establishment is March 9th. First production of aero-engines in Munich. BMW, as a brand, first appeared in 1917. New premises built up in Munich, at the Oberweisenfeld airfield, by 1918

1917 First use of the familiar BMW blue and white emblem based on the Bavarian State colors. BMW develops out of the Rapp company

1923 First production of BMW motorcycles—the flat-twin-cylinder R32—at Milbertshofen

1928 BMW acquired Dixi at Eisenach, began building British Austin Sevens under license

1929 First-ever BMW-badged automobile, the BMW 3/15HP, manufactured at Eisenach

1936 The new Allach factory opened near Munich, meant to concentrate on the building of radial-layout air-cooled aircraft engines

1945 Allach and Milbertshofen (Munich) factories devastated by bombing. Eisenach now behind the "Iron Curtain" and confiscated by the Russians as the occupying power

1951 Launch of the first post-war BMW private automobile—the Type 501 "Baroque Angel" model—in the rebuilt Munich factory

1959 Critical financial crisis, solved by major final investment by the Quandt family

1960 Allach plant (never used for automobile manufacture) partly sold off to MAN. Complete sale achieved later in the 1960s

1962 The first "New Class" car—a 1500 sedan—is launched

1965 Introduction of the 2000CS—first assembly of BMW automobiles by an independent company, Karmann

1966 Financial collapse of the Glas business, in Dingolfing, leading to its takeover by BMW. Modernization and vast expansion then took place. Dingolfing would become BMW's largest single automobile-assembly plant

1969 Transfer of BMW motorcycle manufacture from Munich to the Berlin (Spandau) factory. This became BMW's dedicated two-wheeler plant

1973 Opening of new dedicated BMW assembly plant at Dingolfing
Opening of BMW South Africa at Rosslyn, BMW's first overseas assembly plant

1978 BMW commissioned Lamborghini of Italy to design and engineer the new M1 supercar. Production was intended for Lamborghini, but Lamborghini's financial problems saw this abandoned

1979 Baur of Stuttgart was chosen to assemble M1 supercars
Foundation of the Steyr plant in Austria, for manufacture of BMW gasoline and diesel engines

1986 First BMWs produced at Regensburg, in Germany

1994 BMW completed its first North American assembly plant, at Spartanburg, in South Carolina. From 1995, it became the center of Z3 (later Z4) sports car manufacture, and X5 4x4s were later added to the product mix

1994 BMW absorbed Britain's Rover Group, therefore inheriting the old Longbridge, Oxford, Solihull and Swindon plants

2000 Saddened by inability to make Rover profitable, BMW sold off the business, but retained Oxford (also known as "Cowley") and Swindon to concentrate on new-generation MINI manufacture

2001 The new engine plant at Ham's Hall near Birmingham, England is opened making all BMW's four-cylinder engines from 1600-cc to 2-liter capacity including those for the MINI

2002 A brand-new factory at Goodwood, in England, was opened, to assemble Rolls-Royce automobiles (launched in 2003)

2004 Start of X3 production at the Magna Steyr plant, at Graz, Austria. This is the only BMW vehicle to be produced at a non-BMW owned plant.

2005 New Leipzig factory opened, to assemble 3-Series, and later 1-Series ranges

2007 The completion of the BMW Welt marketing exhibition and museum close to the Munich plant. X3 production moves to Spartanburg.

2008 80th Anniversary of BMW's entry into the automobile-manufacturing business

THE EARLY YEARS

CHAPTER 1

BIRTH, AERO-ENGINES, AND EISENACH

TODAY'S BMW, OF COURSE, IS TOTALLY DIFFERENT from the modest little business that started operating in Munich in 1916, and the famous blue-and-white badge tells its own story. In the beginning, BMW had no interest in automobiles; the company's first products were aircraft engines. Initially, in 1928, they built another company's automobiles—but today around 1.5 million BMW-badged automobiles and motorcycles leave the assembly lines every year. Rolls-Royce and MINI have been added to the company's lists—and who knows how that stable of marques and existing brands might yet grow in the years to come?

The Gustav Otto aircraft factory in Munich about 1912. This unprofitable company was reorganized, by order of the Bavarian War Ministry, on March 9th, 1916 into the Bayerische Flugzeugwerk (BFW) owned by Camillo Castiglioni. When Castiglioni bought back the Bayerische Motoren Werke (BMW) from Knorr-Bremse AG in 1922 he transferred the assets of the BMW company into BFW. The transfer of the name BMW to BFW meant that the former assumed the founding date of the latter —March 9th 1916.

The castle of Wartburg dominates the town of Eisenach.

WARTBURG— WHAT'S IN A NAME?

The Wartburg is a castle mounted on top of a hill that looms over the town of Eisenach, in the Thuringia area of Germany. When the first automobiles came to be built in the town, "Wartburg" was an obvious choice for its name. The castle was founded way back in 1067 by Ludwig der Springer, survived every war and civil disturbance in the area for more than 900 years, and is still an important landmark in this part of the nation. Although home to the Springers for several centuries, it was also noted for having housed Martin Luther for a time in the 16th century. After the Second World War all its ancient and religious artifacts were ruthlessly stripped out by the occupying Russians, and have never been seen again. The castle itself, however, survives to this day.

Way back (well over a hundred years ago) how could anyone have known that the pioneering, crudely-engineered Wartburg—yes, a Wartburg, of all brands, and one that was itself license-built—of 1898 would eventually be one of the distant ancestors of the BMW? That an insignificant town called Eisenach would become the spiritual home of some of Germany's finest automobiles of the period? Was it even conceivable that the original Wartburg model, of which just 85 examples were built in the first two years, would be related to the BMW range, of which millions would follow?

First of all, therefore, this is the very basic development of the family tree:

- There were no BMW-badged machines of any type until 1917—and the very first were aero-engines for German military aircraft.
- The very first BMW-badged road vehicles—to go on flat-twin engined motorcycles—followed in 1923.
- The original BMW-badged private automobile was the BMW 3/15HP of 1929, a mildly-re-engineered license-built Austin Seven. This had already been in production at Dixi, which BMW bought in 1928.

This, however, is to simplify what was a rather complicated development of the pedigree. It is fair to point out that BMW-badged automobiles first appeared in a tentative way, as a result of building other machines under license.

First steps

I must be careful not to trip over the chronology. Although this is an automobile-orientated story, I must never forget that the BMW story itself began with the making of military aircraft engines in Munich. The influence that first led to the building of BMW automobiles came from a long-established business at Eisenach, which was a long way north of Munich, roughly equidistant between Frankfurt in the west, and Leipzig in the east of Germany. Even so BMW, as such, and the Eisenach factory, would not join hands until 1928.

This engineering story therefore begins with a thrusting and resourceful engineer called Heinrich Ehrhardt. By the 1890s Ehrhardt had already set up, expanded, and made much money from several business, before settling down in Eisenach, at the center of the Thuringian economy, and setting up a factory to produce bicycles and military vehicles. The Fahrzeugfabrik Eisenach (Eisenach Vehicle Factory) was set up by 1897, and in 1898 it took space at the Dusseldorf automobile exhibition to show off three types of vehicles: a three-wheeler voiturette (rather like the better-known French Leon Bollee); an electrically-driven coach; and an automobile, which had a rear-mounted 2-cylinder Benz engine and a two-speed gearbox.

Although this original automobile showed promise it was still completely undeveloped, and was quite overshadowed at Eisenach by the bicycles and munitions wagons that flowed out of the plant in ever increasing numbers. Within months, however, Ehrhardt visited Paris, saw much about the latest French Decauville automobile that he liked, and eventually arranged to begin building this 3.5hp machine (which had a top speed of 31mph/50kph) in Eisenach, under license. The new automobile had a new name: Wartburg. It almost chose itself, because the town of Eisenach was overshadowed by the castle of Wartburg—standing high above the town and quite dominating it—of which the Thuringians were extremely proud.

In the next few years, a succession of new Wartburg automobiles were launched, some Decauville-based, others more and more specialized—but they were all relatively expensive, and sold only in small numbers. Despite their high price not even the redoubtable Ehrhardt, who had a long track record of making

Early in its development, BMW relied on the aircraft business for the first few years. BMW's IIIa, IV and V types were all used in the Junkers J F13, the world's first all-metal passenger plane, here seen being assembled at Dessau.

Military requirements during the 1917-1918 period saw the still-young BMW company expand considerably. This was the testing shops at the Moosacherstrasse plant in Munich.

Dated 1918, this shot shows some of the workforce at the burgeoning aircraft engine factory in Munich.

money from his inventions, could make the automobile-building side of this business pay. He eventually withdrew from that business in 1902, just before the "Wartburg" brand name went into hibernation for decades.

Soon afterwards, the resident design team set out to develop a new type of automobile with a smaller engine, and a lower selling price—an automobile that attracted other entrepreneurs and was licensed out for assembly in other factories in other countries. The first of the new automobiles, which went on sale

in 1904, was branded Dixi ("Dixi," incidentally, is Latin for "I have spoken") and soon began to carve out a reputation for itself, and for the Eisenach factory.

The business, even so, could probably not have survived merely by making automobiles—it was bicycles, trucks, and military vehicles that really kept the workforce buzzing. By 1910 more than 1,000 workers streamed in and out of the gates every day; this figure trebled during the First World War as the demand for military material expanded.

Like almost all such engineering factories of a hundred years ago, the premises looked grim and forbidding, both inside and outside, for there were cobbles and setts outdoors, oil and grease on the workshop floor—but the standards of machining and assembly were as high as any in the civilized world. In those days no one—perhaps not even Rolls-Royce—ever expected an automotive chassis to be totally oil-tight, clean, and sparkling for long, but Dixi's standards were as high as most.

Aircraft engines

In the meantime, a company that would shortly become BMW had been set up in the Bavarian capital of Munich, which was more than 200 miles/322 kilometers south of Eisenach and a much bigger and more important location. By this time Germany, at the head of the Central Powers military alliance, had already been involved in an arms race for years and had been fighting the Allies since war broke out in 1914. More and more aircraft were being developed—to fight, to bomb, to reconnoiter, or to transport—and at this time there seemed to be limitless possibilities for a new business to make money. Aero-engine producers Rapp-Motorenwerke succeeded the failed company Flugwerk Deutschland. Founder, Karl Rapp, a senior engineer at Flugwerk Deutschland, took over their premises at 288 Schleisseheimer Strasse in a northern suburb of Munich and established his own company to produce "engines for aircraft and motor vehicles." Rapp gained an order for aero engines from the Marine Flying Corps of the Austro-Hungarian armed forces. In 1916 a commission, led by a young Austrian Naval officer [with mechanical and electrical engineering training], Franz Josef Popp, was sent to Rapp to inspect the engines. A few months later Popp left his duties with the commission and joined Rapp-Motorenwerke as Technical Director. Orders were meagre for Rapp's own products, but the company survived by producing engines under licence for the Austro-Daimler Company. An engineer working at the company, Max Friz, had moved from the Daimler company to Rapp because they had not given sufficient recognition to his designs for a new high altitude aero-engine. Popp recognized the quality of the man's ideas and brought them to the attention of the Prussian military authorities who promptly ordered 600 engines.

The reputation of Rapp-Motoren's own products was poor and it was necessary to form a new company to distance the new production from this reputation. Therefore on July 27,1917 Bayerische Motoren Werke (BMW) was formed out of Rapp-Motorenwerke with Karl Rapp leaving and Popp becoming Managing Director. To fund the company shareholders were invited, including Camillo Castiglioni, an Austrian of Italian descent.

BMW's first aero-engines were built at the Milbertshofen plant in 1917. Following the war Germany was banned from making aero-engines by the Allies and the value of a company like BMW whose main expertise was in making them, dropped to virtually zero. To recoup his considerable investments in the company Castiglioni sold off BMW to Knorr-Bremse AG, a railroad brake manufacturer. However by the 1920s he sensed fresh opportunities for engine manufacture in Germany (aero-engine production was authorized to begin again in 1922) and he bought back BMW together with its well-known company emblem from Knorr-Bremse on June 6, 1922. Castiglioni also owned another aircraft company Bayerische Flugzeigwerk (BFW) which took over the premises of the failing Gustav Otto

Once Eisenach became involved in military machine production, it installed more and more tools. Here is a four-spindle machine in operation in 1919.

By 1910 the Eisenach plant was reaching the limits of its expansion. This drawing was issued in 1910. Thirty years later, BMW's superb late-1930s cars were still being built inside these walls—though many body shells were supplied from outside specialists.

Unser Werk.

Flugmaschinenfabrik (page 13) and he transferred the assets of BMW into BFW.

During the 1920s the production of aero-engines became once again a mainstay of the company. By that time BMW employed more than 3,500 people and was producing in excess of 150 engines every month, which was enough to keep the company going. BMW 6-cylinder and V12-cylinder aero-engines proved themselves in a series of successful long distance test flights.

The sales of truck engines to other companies and flat twin engines also helped. It was at this time that BMW's interest in automobiles, and more critically, motorcycles, was aroused. BMW might never before have built any such machines, but the rapid rise of the automobile had not gone unnoticed. Even so, since this was also a period when Germany came to suffer from

a critical bout of hyperinflation—the worth of its currency was destroyed in a very short time indeed—the miracle was that the company managed to survive in any recognizable form.

Eisenach—and automobiles

In spite of the fact that the BMW business could only stutter along in the mid-1920s, its directors (still led by Castiglioni, and with Franz-Josef Popp now promoted to General Director), kept up their interest in automobiles. Because Castiglioni and several of his fellow directors also had interests in other car companies—notably in the Daimler-Benz combine, whose headquarters were in Stuttgart—it was easy to see where and how this was sustained.

In the meantime, the Dixi business, came to Castiglioni's

Many years after the Eisenach plant was expropriated from BMW, and after the reunification of Germany, the company returned to the town to set up a new plant where a massive new press shop was established to service the rest of the ever-expanding BMW empire.

attention. The rumor, soon converted into credible opinion, was that there in that historic town, and on a very cramped site, was an automotive business that might, just might, be interested in merging its interests with BMW. Amazingly, BMW made their move at what might seem to be exactly the wrong time. Automobile sales in Europe had just reached a 1920s peak, and demand seemed likely to fall. Was this the right time to make a move on another company? Maybe it was, for, looking back, the Fahrzeugfabrik Eisenach operation needed financial help, while BMW, still prosperous in spite of the awful inflation that had afflicted Germany, was looking to break into the automotive industry. Maybe this could be a union blessed by world events?

As already pointed out, the Eisenach plant had begun by making Wartburg automobiles, which were closely related to

French Decauvilles, but these never generated a big demand so in 1904 a new "own-brand" automobile, called Dixi, took over instead. The first Dixis had 1.4-liter 2-cylinder engines; a 4-cylinder 2.5-liter type followed, and a massive 5-liter was then developed—but these still all sold in very small numbers. The automobiles looked good, and were well-engineered, but carried high prices. Even so, with a workforce of a thousand by 1910, this was clearly an important enterprise for what was, after all, still a rather remotely sited township. Like other automobile makers of this period, Dixi then tried to expand in every direction, sometimes using motor sport as a means of advertising their wares. Models with engines as large as 7.0-liters made their appearance; bodywork was as plush and as glossy as any rival in Germany could possible be.

The end of a day's work at Eisenach in 1910, with the workforce pouring out of the factory gates. This factory would still be in use in 1939.

During the First World War, Dixi turned to the manufacture of military trucks and derivatives of their chassis, with the workforce eventually rising to no fewer than 3,100 by the end of the period. As with BMW, the aftermath was both financially and personally painful, for in 1919 the Allied Control Commission demanded the dismantling of a large part of the production facilities. However, within a year, Dixi (whose buildings were, of course, quite un-damaged) was able to start building bicycles and motor vehicles again, though at least a thousand of the workforce had had to be laid off. From 1921, Jacob Schapiro (who, significantly, had business connections with Camillo Castiglioni) took control of the company. He shortly engineered a merger with Gothaer Waggonfabrik AG (a company also controlled by Schapiro, which made it all very easy to arrange!).

The 1920s, which were economically difficult for almost every German concern, made it difficult for the new Gotha-owned Eisenach business, and the company always struggled to sell its automobiles. As another noted historian has written: "Jacob Schapiro, a major stockholder not only of the Gotha factory, but also of Benz, NSU, and various other companies in the motor-vehicle field, was disappointed by the lack of success in Eisenach, and looked for a way out…"

If BMW had not suddenly come upon the scene, Dixi might nevertheless have survived, for in an attempt to boost output at Eisenach, Schapiro then approached Sir Herbert Austin in Britain, proposing to begin making the successful Austin Seven model under license. As we now know, Austin granted the license in a deal sealed in February 1927. Dixi would build the Austin Seven, rebadged it as the Dixi 3/15 Type DA1 (DA = Deutsche Ausfuhrung, or "German Version"), and would be authorized to sell it only in Germany and Eastern Europe. Austin would get a 2 percent royalty on all sales.

This was a masterstroke. After the first batch of 100 automobiles was shipped out, fully built up, from Austin's British factory, Dixi began their "own-brand" manufacture in December 1927 and more than 6,000 automobiles were produced in the calendar year 1928. Four different body styles—sedan, coupe, roadster, and touring automobile, all identical with the British types—were on offer, and this was an automobile that quite transformed the company's prospects. It was no wonder that Schapiro was ready to sell out to BMW, at the right price, before the end of 1928.

CHAPTER 2

POWER FOR THE PEOPLE— MOTORCYCLES IN THE 1920S

IN THE EARLY DAYS—although BMW tried hard to get established in the aircraft engine business—there simply wasn't enough activity to go round, which meant that BMW had to look round for other engineering work to keep them afloat. It was the chance development of a change of company financial backing that then led to them taking their first interest in motorcycles.

BMW R39, R42 and R47
motorcycles lined up, ready for
shipping out, in 1928.

As already noted, financier Camillo Castiglioni sold his shares in BMW in 1920. A year later he took control of BFW, which had succeeded from Gustav Otto's original business, and discovered that immediately after the end of the First World War BFW had been manufacturing motorcycles. Thus it was that in 1922 Castiglioni brought BMW aero-engine manufacture into the BFW factories, which were much under-used. From 1922, the plot of land to the east side of a north-south road called Lerchenauer Strasse, in Munich, was developed into an ever-growing complex, which soon included production halls, a machine shop, and a foundry. The time for building automobiles had still not yet come, but it was there that BMW took the plunge, and decided to make their first road vehicle—a motorcycle.

The early motorcycles

The first BMW two-wheeler—which carried the type number R32—took shape around an all-new engine known as the "Bayern Kleinmotor" (Bavaria Small Engine) and was the very first road vehicle to sport what became the legendary blue-and-white BMW "spinner" logo. Initially, this was to be a 486cc motor, which produced just 8.5 horsepower at 2,800rpm: by twentieth century standards this might sound puny, but by 1920s standards it was extremely competitive, for top speed was almost 60mph/97kph.

Perhaps they did not realize it at the time, but the basic layout of the R32 would establish a template that would keep BMW famous for decades to come. Chief designer Max Friz had looked around the world, analyzed all the possibilities, and settled on a horizontally-opposed flat twin. The original engine, in fact, was the M2B15-type, based on a British Douglas design, and was supplied for fore-and-aft fitment into various other brands of motorcycle (including Victoria, of Nuremberg), but it was an improved type of flat twin that was fitted to the R32. Shaft drive to the rear wheel was also a feature: both these features were retained from generation to generation, so that modern-day BMW owners would have no difficulty in recognizing the historical importance of a 1920s-type two-wheeler when they saw it. It was no accident that the R32's sporting potential was soon obvious, and modified examples were soon seen in racing—and winning too.

When it finally came, the launch of motorcycles signaled a complete revolution in BMW's business, in its image, and of course in the manufacturing facilities that were needed. In 1924 one of the existing buildings (which had produced aero engines)

was first leveled, then replaced by a modern production hall.

The factory was extended and a new foundry added in 1928 so that by the end of the 1920s motorcycle production had become the mainstay of the company's profits. In 1923, just 1,500 motorcycles were built, but by 1927 that figure had risen to 5,000 units! This business continued alongside the thriving aero-engine activities and the company's fledgling ownership of the Dixi car production operation at Eisenach.

By the late 1920s, the company had also built a new test track at one side of the site—actually the northwestern extremity (the green space was rapidly being swallowed up by new industrial developments). The track was a concrete surfaced oval with banked curves, 820 yards/750 meters long, on which the company's newly completed two-wheelers could be tested at up to 90mph/145kph if necessary. This feature would remain until the 1960s—unhappily, it was very visible from the air, and must have proved an ideal aiming point for Allied bombers in the 1940s—but would eventually become redundant, and would be replaced by vast new machine shops and engine assembly lines for "New Class" automobiles.

The existence of this test track (which BMW sometimes coyly described as a "running-in" track) was a real advance, for in earlier years the motorcycles had been tested, very briefly (in conditions quite unthinkable in modern times) indoors! To make the best use of this oval, incidentally, BMW also erected new aero-engine test rigs in the infield. At the same time a short rail spur was added from a nearby main line, which made the company's dispatch arrangements as efficient as possible. Even up until the early 1930s, motorcycles and aero-engines were all manufactured in the same production complex at what became known as the Milbertshofen plant. This was done because there was always a healthy demand for motorcycles, whereas orders for aero-engines came in spasmodically, and in no obvious sequence.

The R32 motorcycle was merely the first of a long series of high-quality two-wheelers for which BMW would soon be famous. The problem, if it was a problem, was that the manufacturing standards, methods, and staffing were always held high, at aero-engine level (many technicians could, and did, work both on motorcycles and aero-engines). This meant that—compared with rivals in Italy and Great Britain—production costs were always high, and that BMW motorcycles were numbered among the most expensive two-wheelers on the market. Not that this seemed to matter, for the clientele was always out there, and profits continued to flow in.

than they became in later years. As far as BMW was concerned this was an ideal product, as it could be assembled in modest halls (at this stage, it was important that the assembly lines and machine shops did not get in the way of the building of large aero-engines), and the only costly machine tools needed were to manufacture the engines and gearboxes. Archive shots show motorcycles taking shape as they moved gradually down simple tracks, positioned at a mechanic's chest level for ease of access.

Soon after the flat-twin R32 had gone on sale, it was joined by the single-cylinder R39 (though the clientele thought it was too expensive), and the twins continued to build on the original model's reputation. At the end of the 1920s, therefore, BMW built a new motorcycle assembly hall to the south of the existing foundry. Even at this stage, please note, there was a modicum of integration between Milbertshofen and the newly-acquired Dixi business at Eisenach (which is described fully in Chapter 3). Motorcycle frames were riveted together from pressed-steel sheet that had been produced at Eisenach, then trucked south through

BMW's first non-aero-engine products were these motorcycles of the 1920s, both machines and factory surroundings looking very different in those days.

The BMW motorcycle division ran a Customer Service School in the 1930s, and this trailer contains the engine and transmission of a BMW R12 motorcycle that circulated the dealer network acting as an aid in training After Sales support staff.

Germany: after being assembled, the frames were then prepared, painted, and added to the lines as the "chassis" of the motorcycles themselves.

Until the late 1930s BMW motorcycles were recognized by their use of pressed-steel frames, but from 1936 the company fell into line with the rest of the world by launching the new 24bhp/494cc R5 type, which had many ultra-modern features. Not only did it use a tubular frame and telescopic front

suspension forks (this was at a time when most of the world's motorcycle industry was still using old-fashioned girder forks and exposed coil springs), but the "boxer" engine now had overhead camshafts, and the four-speed gearbox was foot-operated (though an auxiliary hand control was also retained).

Expansion of the factories

Although BMW had at first assumed that there was plenty of space on the ground for future expansion, this was the 1920s when no-one, nowhere in the world, can have had any idea of how engine-driven machinery—automobiles, motorcycles, commercial vehicles and aircraft—would become such an all-pervasive part of modern life. This meant that in the beginning BMW could never imagine how much space they would eventually expand into around the Milbertshofen site. Luckily the plant was abounded by open fields and by the1930s it was apparent that the plant would need to grow rapidly beyond the present perimeter.

Under plans originally laid down in 1926 (amazingly, such plans still exist, having somehow survived the bombing that would follow within twenty years), plots of land in the southeastern corner of the site (those, in fact, which were closest to the center of Munich) were purchased. This is where a U-shaped group of factory buildings were established, mainly for the machining and assembly of aero-engines, while motorcycle construction was concentrated north of them, closer to the test track. At this time, it seems, there were never any plans to start building automobiles in Munich. Not only would there have been a distinct lack of space, but also BMW took the very practical view that all the four-wheeler expertise was developing at Eisenach, where they hoped it would stay. Until the earth-shattering events of 1939–45 changed Europe's political and geographical map for ever, that view did not change. Later in the 1930s, the last "green space" at Milbertshofen was eliminated, since new buildings—small, large or massively re-developed—gradually crept across the site, and another block was built on land to the north of the original northern boundary (Keferloherstrasse) where the BMW Flugmotoren GmbH used it for aero-engine purposes. It returned to BMW AG ownership in 1947 as the bomb-damaged sites were gradually being cleared and restored.

During the 1930s, therefore, BMW's business expanded mightily on three entirely different paths. Due to a flow of military orders, the aero-engine side (as we shall see in Chapter 4) became more and more important, the company's

By 1910, Dixi cars were being
assembled at Eisenach by
traditional means. There was no
question of a moving assembly line
being needed, and much fettling
and fitting was needed to get the
cars ready for bodies to be added.

By 1910, Dixi cars were being assembled at Eisenach by traditional means. There was no question of a moving assembly line being needed, and much fettling and fitting was needed to get the cars ready for bodies to be added.

First of all, Camillo Castiglioni recognized the worth of a sporty new 4-cylinder automobile at Austro-Daimler, which had been designed by a talented engineer called Dr. Ferdinand Porsche. This was the same Porsche, of course, who would later go on to even greater things, by designing the VW Beetle, and whose bureau would also be responsible for the Auto-Union P-Wagen, the original Porsche sports car, and (during the 1940s) for some formidable military tanks. The redoubtable Porsche, however, rejected the very idea of that automobile ever being built in Munich, as it was abandoned.

Next there was the idea of producing a small front-wheel-drive automobile around a Czechoslovakian Tatra tubular chassis, with a 500cc horizontally-opposed engine, a three-speed transmission, and exposed front drive shafts. Nothing came of that, nor did the evolution of an automobile known as the Schwabische Huttenwerke-Kamm, which had a very similar front-wheel-drive layout—this time with a water-cooled engine and a pioneering type of unit-construction body structure. In spite of a lack of resources BMW was never short of enterprise, but although three prototypes were made the Kamm project had

The Eisenach factory complex, photographed in 1929, the year in which the first BMW-badged cars took to the roads. Surrounded by public highways, there was no space for further expansion of premises.

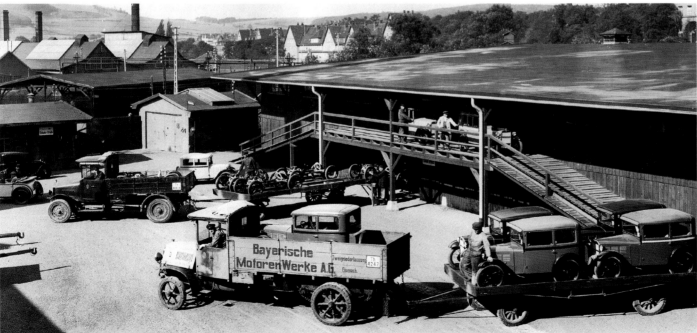

This is one of the remaining archive studies of the dispatch of the original BMW cars, the BMW3/15HPs, from Eisenach in 1929. It was a modest beginning, but progress thereafter was rapid.

In spite of the advanced engineering for which BMW would soon be known world-wide, in 1929 the service/repair buildings at Eisenach still looked amazingly rustic.

OPPOSITE
By the time the BMW 3/15, which had evolved from the Austin Seven, was announced, BMW also had an assembly plant at Berlin-Johannisthal.

to be dropped in 1927. At this stage, it was not certain that BMW would ever progress to making automobiles. New financial capital was available by 1928, but most of this was earmarked for the aero-engine side of the business. At an extraordinary meeting held in mid-1928, the decision was formally made to abandon the Kamm automobile.

The acquisition of Eisenach

Although several speeches at the extraordinary meeting expressed interest in starting to build automobiles, the directors made no concrete commitments. The board, in fact, was split— with Castiglioni all in favor, but colleagues resisting him. It was

only after Castiglioni had talked long and hard to other board members that Dr Von Stauss, the President of the BMW Supervisory Board, and Managing Director, Franz Josef Popp were persuaded to support the idea of building automobiles. Knowing that the Gotha-owned Dixi business in Eisenach was in trouble, Castiglioni went off to the Thuringian town to strike a deal with the company. His objective was not only to take control of the company, but to get his hands on a new automobile that they were assembling—the Austin Seven-based Dixi 3/15. If BMW were not to be encouraged to design their own first automobile, he would annex one that was already on sale.

It was Jacob Schapiro (who was financially involved in

THE AUSTIN SEVEN

Every automotive enthusiast, surely, knows that the Dixi 3/15 was no more than a lightly modified, license-built British Austin Seven—but how many know that this little automobile was the model that saved Austin from bankruptcy in the early 1920s? Herbert Austin had set up shop at Longbridge, near Birmingham, England, in 1905, had built hundreds, not thousands, of large and medium-sized automobiles before the First World War, expanded mightily during the conflict, then found himself with a vast, near-empty complex in 1919. A newly launched 20/4 was not a success, but after Austin retreated to his home with one young designer, Stanley Edge, to engineer a new small automobile, the business was saved.

First on sale in 1923, the Austin Seven was an astonishing success, and would sell in big numbers until the end of the 1930s. The combination of a simple chassis frame, transverse leaf spring suspension for the axles, a sturdy side-valve 747cc engine, a three-speed gearbox and cable-operated rear wheel brakes, was cheap and easy to make. Prices were low, there were several different body styles—and although this was only one of several automobiles in the company's range, Austin's future was assured.

Austin suddenly became a desirable property, but although several takeover approaches were made (one, notably, from General Motors, who finally bought Vauxhall instead), Herbert Austin contented himself with licensing out the Austin Seven for other companies to build. Dixi, needing a small automobile to sell in a still-impoverished German market, were the first (followed by Rosengart in France), and re-named "their" automobile the Dixi 3/15, and for a time Bantam (in the United States) would follow suit. Although the Dixi 3/15 was phased out soon after BMW's purchase in favor of the BMW 3/15, and later the BMW 3/20, Austin Seven assembly in the United Kingdom carried on until 1939, with nearly 300,000 examples built.

several German industrial concerns of the period, not least Daimler-Benz and Gotha!), who acted as an honest broker. A merger deal came together with great speed in the summer and autumn of 1928, and by the end of the year BMW was in complete control of the Eisenach premises: in March 1929 the Eisenach Court of Register made public this entry: "From henceforth [the Eisenach Vehicle Factory becomes] the Eisenach subsidiary of the Bavarian Motor Works AG…" Although BMW would expand even more in the 1930s (the evolution of a brand-new aero-engine factory at Allach, in the suburbs of Munich was a perfect example), henceforth, and for the next seventeen years, BMW's empire would have two major bases—one at Milbertshofen, Munich, the other at Eisenach. Although

Eisenach's floor area was quite dwarfed by that of Milbertshofen (Allach, with widely dispersed buildings, was bigger than both of them), the BMW car products that began flowing out of Eisenach attracted much attention and admiration. By 1939, when the Second World War broke out, more than 4,500 people were working at Eisenach.

When BMW management moved into Eisenach to start imposing their own ideas, they found that the business was thriving. The assembly line was already full of stubby little automobiles that were really no more and no less than re-badged British Austin Sevens. Every week more than 150 of these modest little machines, badged as Dixi 3/15s—many of them with open-top bodywork—would roll out of the gates. Of the

The very first BMW-badged car
was this tiny four-cylinder engined
3/15hp car of 1929. Things would
change dramatically in the next ten
years.

OPPOSITE LEFT
Right from the start, BMW
machined all the forgings and
castings needed to produce its
machinery. How many vehicles
could be served by this stack of
crankshafts?

German-designed Dixi models, however—the 1,568cc 6/24, the 2,354cc or 3,557cc P1/P2 types, or the 2,354cc 9/40 types—there was virtually no sign, as these were expensive and technically ordinary automobiles that no longer appealed to the public. Nor, it seemed, did Dixi currently have much in mind to replace them in the marketplace. BMW, for their part, did not really mind this. It was used to selling cheaper machinery (the motorcycles, though expensive as bikes, were none-the-less cheaper than Dixi automobiles) and maybe the Austin Seven-based automobile was not glamorous, but it was the right automobile at the right time, and could be marketed through the Dixi dealer network. Not only that, but it was priced at the

lowest of all bargain basements levels in a country that was still recovering from the hyperinflation of the mid-1920s. Those were the days when Dixi 3/15 prices started at RM 2,750 (about $650) with the most vigorous domestic competition coming from DKW, Hanomag, and Opel.

In modern parlance, to get their show on the road and design their own new product would take time, capital, and a fresh start. The engineers were available, but time was not. BMW's first pragmatic move was therefore to turn the Dixi 3/15 into the BMW-Dixi 3/15 at once—without any technical changes. This happened effective January 1, 1929. The next move, only seven months later in July 1929, was to introduce a modified version

The metal fitters' shop at Eisenach in the early 1930s shows evidence of in-house production of body shell pressings.

Loading a BMW 320 Convertible body into the paint shop, in Eisenach, in 1937.

that finally dropped the Dixi name. This was known as the BMW 3/15HP (Type DA 2), and was really the source of all later BMW automobiles. It was a model range very similar to the original Dixi, but with larger and more capacious bodies, modified front grilles, a choice of coachwork (including an all-steel sedan shell from Ambi-Budd of Berlin), and four-wheel brakes.

To match the competition (Opel in particular) prices had been reduced—they now started at RM 2,200 (about $525)—but BMW's ambitions were clear. Interestingly, in 1930 there was a Type DA3 version of this automobile, with 18bhp instead of 15bhp, a two-seater sports tourer type of body, and the model name of "Wartburg." Management local to Eisenach were still proud of the castle that dominated the town—and, in its day, this seemed to be a capable little machine. The last derivative, the DA4 of 1931, was controversially equipped with swing-axle front suspension, and did not seem to handle as well.

Happily, the 3/15HP kept BMW's production lines busy until 1932. In this period, BMW transformed a factory that needed business, to one that needed more space in which to operate—and if that sounds familiar, think of the Glas take over of 1966, which signaled the same effect. The factory, at this time, could

not be much modified, but was smartened up, and made as efficient as possible. By 1932, no fewer than 9,308 Dixi 3/15s, and 15,948 BMW 3/15s had been produced. Management, though, had never seen these automobiles as being important to BMW's future, but rather as a modest little beginning that could keep the business ticking over, and the cash registers ringing.

The development of the 3/20

The last Dixi-badged automobile had been built in the summer of 1929, and now the last Dixi/Austin-engined BMW left the assembly lines in 1932, for the 3/20 that then took over was very different indeed. Here was a much more technically advanced automobile, more spacious, and easily shrugging off the last vestiges of a British parentage. Although it was still a tiny "3hp" automobile (according to contemporary German taxation rules), and cost from only RM 2650 ($630), it showed the way that BMW's engineers were thinking—and were allowed to think, for what they developed was certainly not the cheapest way of doing anything.

The new chassis was now a sturdy backbone, front, and rear suspension were both now independent (by transverse leaf springs) but, most important of all, although the engine had a similar bulk to the Austin Seven, this time it had a stroke of 80mm instead of 76mm, and was a brand-new overhead-valve 4-cylinder type of 782cc, which developed 20bhp. To those in the know, behind-the-scenes co-operation with Daimler-Benz showed through, for the new all-steel sedan body was produced in D-B's own plant at Sindelfingen, a suburb of Stuttgart (this, incidentally, being the same much-changed site which assembles Mercedes-Benz automobiles to this day).

Sales ticked over steadily, with 7,215 automobiles being sold before this model was dropped in mid-1934. Viewed on its own, the engine might not be considered all that significant, but when I point out that a 6-cylinder evolution, which would use some common components (including the same bore and stroke dimensions) already figured in BMW/Eisenach's master plans, it makes more sense.

Though the world-wide Depression hit Germany with a rare ferocity in 1931/1932, BMW kept their nerve and pressed ahead with yet another new automobile: the BMW303, which appeared in February 1933. By this time, BMW had a 6 percent market share of German sales—making them fifth in the ever-changing pecking order—the Nazi party had just come in to power in Germany, the country's economy began to pick up, and BMW's ambition soon became apparent.

A suitable celebration for the building of the 25,000th BMW 3/15 model. This historic moment took place at Eisenach in September 1931. This figure included all Dixi and BMW 3/15HP sales from 1927 to 1931.

Even though World War Two had already broken out, in 1940 BMW found time to produce a team of ultra-special coupe versions of the BMW 328 model, which dominated the Italian Mille Miglia race.

Although BMW did not always like to allow individuals to generate towering personal reputations such as the automobiles themselves had, from the summer of 1932 an important new automotive engineer, Dipl. Eng. Fritz Fiedler, arrived at Eisenach to become chief designer. Fiedler was already much respected for his reputation with two other German concerns—Stoewer, and also Horch—and he would soon have an influence on many BMW automobiles to be produced in the next generation. Incidentally, Fiedler would unwittingly become a factor in the "war reparations" captured by D.A. Aldington of Britain's AFN, for when the design of the 6-cylinder engine was moved to England, Fiedler moved with it. He would soon be noted for his work in England on the Bristol automobiles and engines that followed.

In the years that followed, from the launch of the 303, to the building of the last pre-Second World War civil-market BMW 335 of 1941, the company would take what we now call "product planning" to a fine art. In eight seasons, there would be only three entirely different types of chassis for the private automobiles, small or not-so-small, brisk or fast, but each automobile would use a version of what we now call the "kidney" radiator grille, and all of them would set standards that rivals could often not match. All of them featured independent front suspension by transverse leaf springs, and all but the last of all (the 335, which had a new, large, power unit) would use one or other derivation, or more powerful, version of

the modern 4-cylinder/6-cylinder engine family.

Throughout this time, the Eisenach factory gradually became more and more full of machinery and workmen, although the site itself could no longer be expanded as it was surrounded by roads and other properties. Military aero-engine activity eventually arrived in Eisenach, but in another factory erected some distance out of town. As to the automobiles, gradually they became faster, even better equipped, ever more stylish, and (because they were quite costly) sold steadily but not sensationally fast.

The original BMW 303-generation automobiles (1933–37) all used one or other version of a tubular chassis frame, with a beam rear axle that rode on half-elliptic springs. Later automobiles—the 320-generation types of 1937–41—had more sturdy box-section chassis frames and, depending on the model, either half-elliptic leaf springs or longitudinal torsion bars to support their rear axles. Finally, and most significantly as far as BMW's sporting reputation was concerned, the rare, exotic, and very desirable 328 two-seater was one on its own, for it had a tubular chassis frame which was matched to half-elliptic rear leaf springs. Most important of all, though, was the engine, the smooth long stroke "six," which would give such sturdy and reliable service, though extensively modified and developed, until

the late 1950s. Although it all started as an innocuously specified 30bhp power unit, by the 1950s it had grown in size, and tripled its peak output.

Although I have published the chart that follows on other occasions, it still tells, succinctly, the way in which BMW's Dr. Fiedler turned something worthy into something quite remarkable. This is how production, at Eisenach, progressed:

Year Introduced (and the first BMW model to use it)	Capacity (cc)	Bore and Stroke (mm)	Peak power bhp/rpm
1933 (303)	1,173	56 × 80	30/4000
1934 (315)	1,490	58 × 94	34/4000
1935 (319)	1,911	65 × 96	45/3750
1936 (326)	1,971	66 × 96	50/3750
1936 (328)	1,971	66 × 96	80/5000
1955 (501/3)	2,077	68 × 96	72/4500

Engineers always find it fascinating to see how such a considerable "stretch" in an engine's cubic capacity can be achieved in what looks like an easy manner. Be assured that unless an engine was vastly over-engineered in the first place, then it is never easy! In the case of the legendary BMW "six,"

Adolf Hitler, flanked by Fritz Hille, Hermann Goering, Franz Josef Popp and Adolf Hünlein, inspecting BMW's latest pride and joy, the 327/28 model, at the IAMA show in Berlin in 1938.

ABOVE LEFT
Although 1930s BMWs were technically advanced vehicles, their assembly details were still very simple. Here, at Eisenach, 320-type bodies take shape in the body shop.

BMW developed special-bodied version of the already-successful 326 chassis, and intended to market it as the 332. Here, in 1940, is a streamlined prototype example. The project did not survive the fighting, and only two cars are known to have survived.

TOP RIGHT
BMW 321 assembly, at Eisenach, in 1939. Note the latest type of transverse leaf independent front suspension. The 321 range, manufactured under Soviet control, would be the main post-war product at Eisenach for some years in the late 1940s.

over the years, the cylinder bore dimension went up by 12mm/0.47in., while that of the stroke went up by 16mm/0.63in. Even so, this was enough to allow the capacity to grow by no less than 77 percent. If there is any failing here, it is that every derivative was a long-stroke power unit, which meant that most of them were strong on low-speed torque, but limited as to how high they could be revved for sporting purposes.

A sporty automobile

It took time to establish BMW's reputation for sporty automobiles. The original 303 and the (4-cylinder) 309 types were very worthy, but without much performance: with a mere 30bhp from 1,173cc, the 303 could only reach 56mph/90kph. This all changed in 1935, with the arrival of the BMW 315/1 and 319/1 Roadsters of 1934 and 1935. Not only was the engine being allowed to develop some of the power that was hidden away inside it—the BMW 319/1 had 55bhp and 1,911cc, and the automobile itself could reach 81mph/130kph—but they had

attractive two-seater styles too. And, can you see some of the styling cues that were carried forward to the sensational 328, which followed a year later?

The BMW 326 range of 1936—sedans and cabriolets—were fine automobiles with box-section ladder-type chassis, and 50bhp/1971cc engines (Autenrieth of Darmstadt produced the open-top and closed coupe body shells, as they would do for later-1930s BMW too), but that was the year in which the splendid BMW 328 two-seater caused such a stir. Quite simply, it was the transformation of the engine that caused such a fuss. Yes, it all happened more then seventy years ago, so at that range (and with modern, jaundiced eyes, who would expect much more) it is difficult to see why an 80bhp/1971cc-engined sports car should cause such a fuss. Simple. At the time this was the best-handling, best-looking, and somehow the "purest" BMW automobile yet made. The earlier 315/319 pedigree combination of a tubular chassis frame with transverse leaf independent front suspension, was retained, weight was pared, the style was advanced—and the 1971cc engine had been transformed. With a new cylinder head, part-spherical combustion chambers, and complex cross-pushrod valve actuation, the engine was a 1930's masterpiece. Even then, in racing form BMW coaxed more than 120bhp from it—by the 1950s Bristol had produced well over 140bhp.

Although the 328 was undeniably expensive—the complete Roadster retailed at RM 7400 in Germany (the equivalent of about $1,750)—no-one suggested that it wasn't worth it. Of its day, it had everything—good looks, a soft ride, powerful hydraulic brakes, independent front suspension and a near-100mph/160kph top speed. No-one, it seemed, could offer more. In some ways, though, this was a pre-Second World War peak of BMW's achievements, for they, like other automobile manufacturers in the German motor industry, were already distracted by the demands of the coming war. Although Hitler kept on saying that he did not want war, no-one with any sense believed him, and an analysis of the new automobiles, trucks, tanks, and aircraft being designed all told another story.

BMW had the new Allach factory to cosset (see Chapter 4), and a new four-wheel-drive Type 325 "scout" automobile to finalize. This meant that the 328, the 55bhp 327 coupes and roadsters which followed in 1937, and the excellent 327/28 of 1938 (the big attraction of this automobile was the use of the 328's 80bhp engine) had not really got into their stride when the Second World War broke out and the civilized world changed—for ever.

If Germany had carried on in a peaceful fashion, BMW's all-new 335 of 1939 might have made its mark. The engineers, for sure, were certainly proud of it. It was much larger than earlier BMWs, with a bigger 90bhp/6-cylinder 3,485cc engine. With a 90mph/145kph top speed, a sturdy box-section chassis frame, and in six-light four-door sedan, it was offered for only RM 6700 (approximately $1,600), in great style and comfort. Unhappily it came along too late—only 410 such automobiles were built, the last batch being for military use in 1941—and it would not be revived in 1945. And that, as far as peacetime motoring was concerned, was that, for after September 1, 1939, BMW transformed itself into an efficient producer of weapons of war, particularly the thousands of magnificent air-cooled radial aero-engines which I cover in the next chapter.

And now, the statistics. Between 1928 and 1941, nearly 79,000 BMW-badged automobiles had left that plant, which even at a peak rate of around 8,000 automobiles a year sounds creditable enough—though that figure would eventually be dwarfed by post-war achievements. What BMW did between 1939 and 1945 was even more remarkable.

Safety first! In the machine shop at Eisenach, a large poster, showing a skull, warns: "Every careless move can be fatal. Take care!"

In 1940, the Type 385 only progressed as far as this full-size clay model. The project would not be revived in later years.

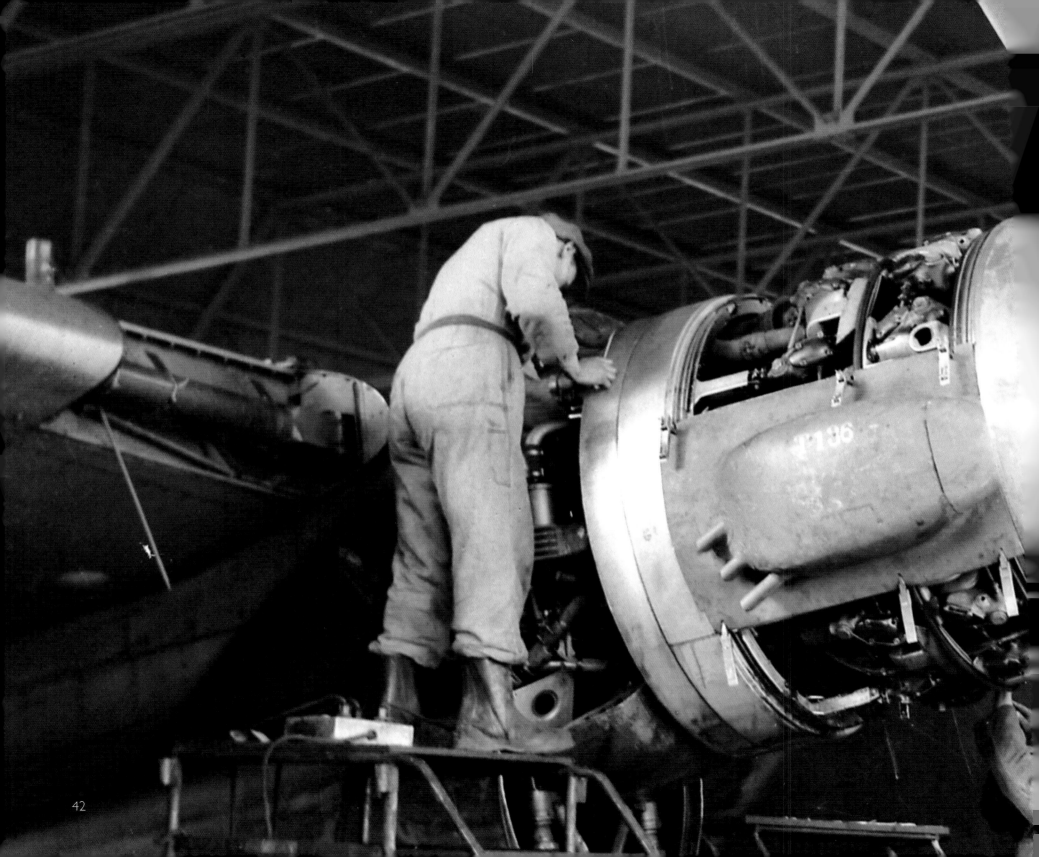

INTO BATTLE

CHAPTER 4

NEW FACTORIES
AND
NEW AERO-ENGINES

IN THOSE FORMATIVE DECADES, it is still too easy to underestimate just how important the aircraft engine side of the fast-growing business had become. Without a steady build up of interest in BMW's aircraft engines, not least from the Germany military, the rest of the company might possibly not have been viable at times.

Complete with its double-row radial BMW 801 air-cooled engine, the Focke-Wulf Fw 190 fighter aircraft was superior to any Allied fighter for some time during the Second World War.

As the 1930s progressed, BMW expanded its factories in Munich, and prepared to build a series of super-powerful aero engines. This was also a time when BMW apprentices were encouraged to join the Hitler youth programme.

Working with Pratt & Whitney

The business link between the first BMW motorcycles (1923) and the first automobiles (1929) has already been described, but it was really an American aircraft engine building concern—Pratt & Whitney—who sparked off further phenomenal advances. The breakthrough came in 1928 when that leading manufacturer granted a license to BMW to build two air-cooled radial layout engines, the 525hp 9-cylinder Hornet aero-engine, and the smaller type 450hp Wasp and 300hp Wasp Junior engines. By the standards of the day, the Hornet and Wasp were completely state-of-the-art, for they had die-cast duralumin crankcases, two-piece crankshafts, steel cylinder barrels, and light alloy cylinder heads. Large in diameter, they were cooled by the blast of air coming back from the propellers, but because of their radial layout they were very short (fore and aft), though wide, and were easily packaged into modern wings and fuselages. They were compact, sturdy, and immensely potent and it was from them that BMW learned, and learned rapidly, how to make improvements.

BMW soon began to evolve their own designs, of which the phenomenal Type 801 was at the pinnacle. The result was that by the 1940s BMW's radial engines, single row or twin row types, all developed—a long way developed—from the Hornet and Wasp types, had become formidable and reliable power units. Used, in particular, in fighter planes as fast as the famous Focke-Wulf Fw190 fighter, their performance was feared by every one of the Allied air forces.

However, even before the Pratt & Whitney designs went into production at Milbertshofen in 1929, it was BMW's own-brand of water-cooled engines that had made a reputation. The first successful aero-engine model was the water-cooled 6-cylinder BMW IIIa and IV types, this soon being followed by a massive 12-cylinder BMW VI, which had evolved by "doubling up" the IV. The VI was so successful that, having been put on test beds for the first time in 1924, it remained in production until 1937 and 6,000 units were manufactured. And although the P & W-derived radial engines soon became BMW "flagship" products, there was also time for small "own-brand" 5-cylinder radials (of 2.17-liters and 2.92-liters) to be made. It was, however, BMW's reputation in providing big engines for massive Luftwaffe transports like the Junkers JU52 (which used the BMW 132 of 685hp), which secured the company's reputation.

Further expansion

As already explained, by the mid-1930s, the Milbertshofen plant in Munich had been expanded, transformed, and built towards the very limit of its original capability and expanded by buying up much of the available land surrounding the complex. To this day those public roads have limited any further growth, and is only in recent years that the fabulous new BMW Welt (BMW World) building has broached those barriers on the southwestern edge of the complex. Within those boundaries, motorcycles of all types and aircraft engines were the staple products, for even at this time all BMW automobiles were being produced at the Eisenach plant. Factory historians insist that the only automobiles built in Milbertshofen before 1952 were experimental vehicles, constructed in the development workshops. Even so, further expansion became necessary. Accordingly, from 1934, a new subsidiary company, BMW Flugmotoren GmbH, was set up, land was purchased to the north of the original block (north of Keferloher Strasse) and expansion continued. However, by the time the war broke out in 1939, this sprawling factory had reached its limits, and was already as large as it would remain for the remainder of the century.

From 1933 onwards, the political dominance of the National Socialist (Nazi) regime made an increasing impact on Germany's

Adolf Hitler, flanked by Franz Josef Popp, inspecting aircraft engine crankshaft housings on a visit to Munich in 1935.

In the 1940s, BMW's Type 801 radial engine was a mighty power unit, produced in large numbers. This 1940 shot shows an impressive line up of connecting rods, close to a milling machine in the Allach center.

In the late 1930s, and at the behest of the military authorities, BMW built a brand-new aero-engine factory at Allach, some distance from Munich, making sure that it was well-camouflaged, and hidden in mature trees.

industries, for it came to need more and more military machinery of every type. Along with Daimler-Benz, BMW found themslves becoming one of the government's favored suppliers of aero-engines—originally of two different types: the tried-and-tested water-cooled BMW VI and the then-new air-cooled BMW 132 radial. Amazingly, the commercial links with Pratt & Whitney of North America not only survived this politically turbulent period, but actually became stronger. Like almost every American citizen and organization, P & W was slow to see the menace that was gradually, but inexorably, growing in Germany, and so saw no reason to withhold information on their own

products if there was a profit to be made. Although the original license deal had lapsed in 1931 a new deal was sealed in 1933, which soon resulted in P & W's Type SD42 being modified by BMW and marketed as the Type 132, this eventually producing up to 1,000hp.

There was, however, a limit to what could be achieved at Milbertshofen, especially after the Reich Aviation Ministry issued an edict to BMW in 1936 stating that they should immediately stop all work on military-type water-cooled engines, and concentrate on making bigger, better and more powerful air-cooled radial engines, in larger quantities. Chief executive Franz Josef Popp was delighted to receive these instructions, for he had long been a fan of the company's radials—but he needed a new plant in which to carry the orders out. It was at this juncture that BMW developed another site—still in the northwestern suburbs of Munich—called Allach, which was originally financed by funds from the state. Although this was only a few miles to the west of Milbertshofen itself, it was a heavily wooded area, and until 1945 (when it was taken over by the liberating American forces) it was always destined to remain so. There was no artistic or conservation reasoning behind this, but rather practical considerations. Because the Allach plant was always intended to produce military engines, the buildings were to be camouflaged (the main halls were also to be widely separated, one from another, to mitigate the effect of the bombing that must surely follow), and some of the site would be developed underground. Colloquially this was known within the country as a "forest factory" (the British equivalent was a "shadow" factory—not invisible, but acting in parallel with established

RIGHT
Component and sub-assembly manufacture of the mighty Type 801 engine in 1941, in Hallein, which was a dispersal plant for the bomb-damaged Milbertshofen plant.

OPPOSITE
When fitted with two BMW Type 801 A radial aero engines, the Dornier Do 217E was a formidable bomber during the Second World War.

BELOW
Complete with its double-row radial BMW 801 air-cooled engine, the Focke-Wulf Fw 190 fighter aircraft was superior to any Allied fighter for some time during the Second World War.

aero-engine manufacturers), and it soon took much of BMW's attention.

Franz Josef Popp was always proud of Allach, christening it the "Reich Works," and if Germany had been victorious in the conflict that followed it would most certainly have become a more important factory than Milbertshofen, because it was so spacious. Incidentally, it was in connection with this expansion that BMW soon took over the business of the Brandenburg Motor Works (or "Bramo") at Spandau in Berlin. Like BMW, Bramo had been building and developing air-cooled aero-engines (including the 14-cylinder double-radial engine, the Bramo 329), and it was after pressure from the RAM that BMW closed down that program, and set Spandau to become a satellite version of the new Allach factory instead. To help supply the land-locked Spandau plant, further factories were also built close by, at Basdorf and at Zuhlsdorf.

Originally, at Allach, the factory was used for assembling and testing Type 132 radial engines, and their developments, but before long, complete manufacture began to take place, and by the early 1940s the legendary Type 801 radial engine was being made both at Allach and at Milbertshofen. To give a guide to the expansion which had taken place, 257 units had been built in 1931, but 1,986 engines were produced in 1939—and this was still before the Munich plants had completely given themselves over to the Type 801 range of engines.

The events of the Second World War

Surprisingly, Allach escaped the worst of the allied bombing attacks that followed (Milbertshofen, as we shall see, was systematically flattened by the USAAF and British RAF bomber fleets between 1942 and 1945), and by the end of the Second World War would be employing no fewer than 17,000 workers, many of them from nearby concentration camps built at Dachau. Forced labor and foreign workers became a great feature of the operation—the figures show that at least 10,000 were employed by the end of 1942, for many able-bodied German men were drafted into the services to fight and had to be replaced.

As the Second World War developed, BMW's activities were speedily subsumed to the desires of the state—and particular to the needs of the military planners. After 1939, a diminishing number of automobiles were completed at Eisenach—mainly for delivery to those whose mobility was considered vital to state business. However, this Thuringian factory also produced 3,225 four-wheel-drive Type 325s for use as scout automobiles: these machines had 50bhp/1,971cc engines, detuned from those also

THE BMW 801 AERO-ENGINE

Although inspired by the Pratt & Whitney Hornet and Wasp aero-engines, which BMW had secured a license to manufacture, the famous BMW 801 was totally designed, in detail, by BMW itself. Work on this project began at the end of 1938, and the very first prototype ran in April 1939. Thereafter the 801 became the only twin-row radial engine to be produced in Germany throughout the Second World War.

The 801 aero-engine was a massive piece of engineering, with 14 cylinders in two rows of seven, each with a bore and stroke of 6.14in/156mm, and a capacity of 2,552 CID/41.8 liters. Supercharging, and the use of fuel injection, were two features of every original derivative; exhaust-driven turbochargers were added at a later date, and naturally the peak power output increased steadily as the war progressed. Original 801s—the 801A, 801B and 801C types—produced 1,600bhp, which at the time was well in excess of even more famous engines such as the Rolls-Royce Merlin. When modified to run on high-octane fuel, peak power rose to 1,730bhp, and when water-ethanol injection was also added, peak power rose to 2,000bhp. A 2,400bhp derivative was under development at the end of the fighting, and by this time the "high-altitude" versions were much superior to anything being deployed by the Allied air forces.

Although it was the Focke-Wulf Fw190 fighter and the Junkers JU88 bombers that brought most fame to the 801, there were many other successful applications. 801 production was in full swing to the very end of hostilities, but the project was then killed off, and never revived.

used in private automobiles like the 326 and 327. Motorcycle production carried on full blast at Milbertshofen before being moved to Eisenach in 1942. By then Milbertshofen had turned itself over completely to the test, development, and manufacture of Type 801 aero-engines in place of the ageing Type 132 radial. Hidden away in the forests just a short distance away the Allach plant produced nothing but aero-engines.

After the first major bombing raid of March 1943 had caused major damage to the original plant, BMW were forced to disperse their activities far and wide, into small premises requisitioned all around Munich—almost all of them within 43 miles/70 kilometers of the Milbertshofen factory. This relocation was complete by mid-1944, and was not only mirrored by other major German businesses (notably Daimler-Benz), but by many similar factories in Great Britain.

Even though aero-engine production was much disrupted in 1944 and 1945 by further large scale bombing raids, Type 801 engines continued to be built, and their performance continued to improve. In many ways, this was of great value to BMW when it strove to recover after 1945, for much of the light-alloy metal in stock—either as raw material or as finished components—could be recovered and reused to make cooking pans.

In the meantime, there was one other top secret strategy that BMW developed throughout the war years—the design, development, and refinement of jet and rocket engines. At that time, many British and American observers assumed that the jet programs originated by Frank Whittle in England, and subsequently put into production by Rolls-Royce, were world leaders—but they were not. BMW, and other specialist engine builders in Germany, were also racing to prepare jet engines of their own, and if the fortunes of war had swung the other way, it is certain that these would have played a bigger part. As it was, the test and development sections involved were over-run in April 1945, and the programs came to nothing.

What followed in the late 1940s, especially in terms of political wrangles and geographical ambitions, brought BMW to the brink of extinction. Who would have thought that the company would lose the Eisenach factory for ever, and that its first post-war automobile would not be delivered for seven years?

REBIRTH

CHAPTER 5

LOSING EISENACH, BUILDING UP MUNICH

B Y 1945, DUE TO THEIR PROMINENT involvement in building aero-engines, the BMW factories had been badly damaged in the Allied bombing raids. This made the company's future seem bleak indeed. Unfortunately as it turned out, their flattened factories were not the only thing in the way of them starting up again. Political and military storm clouds gathering would give rise to a situation in which what was left of their machinery would be confiscated and the Eisenach plant would end up behind the Iron Curtain.

From 1943 to 1945 the Allied bombing offensive was relentless. Although the Allach complex survived, virtually unscathed, the Milbersthofen factory was severely damaged. This is just one corner of the devastation which took place in March 1943.

Although the Russian authorities revived the Eisenach plant after 1945, it had not been much damaged during the war, and there was little new post-war investment. This study, dating from 1948, could easily have been from the mid-1930s, for little has changed.

No sooner had the worst of the winter snows melted in the first weeks of 1945, than the Allies began their final squeeze on the German forces. From the east, the Russians soon encircled Berlin, and pressed ahead to meet the Americans, who had crossed the Rhine in March. In the meantime, a recent summit meeting at Yalta, had established post-war occupation zones. Munich, it seemed, would be in the zone to be administered by American forces, aero-engine (soon to be motorcycle) facilities in Berlin would come under all four of the occupying powers, while Eisenach (the pre-war center of BMW private-automobile production) would find itself just inside the Russian zone. So far, so good, but before the fighting stopped, the armored spearheads of the American divisions had swept over these self-imposed borders before meeting each other. Eisenach, for instance, found itself already at least 100 miles/160 kilometers behind the American front line. When the American forces marched into BMW's various factories in April 1945, as expected they found desolate, under-manned, premises that were shabby, down-at-heel, damaged, and not at all ready to take up a peaceful life

again. Nor were they producing much military material, and the workforce, long weary of the fighting, was now defiantly looking forward to re-construction, and a rebuilding of civilized existence, to begin.

Post-war restructuring

For BMW, all might eventually have been well if Eisenach had found itself permanently in the American zone, but it did not. Political decisions had already been made, which ensured that the Russian zone would include the Thuringia region: this included the town of Eisenach, and the BMW factories that were its main employer. Though General Patton's Third Army had originally liberated the region by May 1945, within weeks these forces were obliged to draw back to previously-agreed Zone boundaries. These were agonizing days for the citizens of Eisenach, who had no say in what transpired. Though they were only about 6 miles/10 kilometers from what became the border—yes, really, that close—and a mere 50 miles/80

OPPOSITE
After the fighting was over, in 1945 the Eisenach factory found itself in the East Occupation Zone, and controlled by the Russians. The new owners began to manufacture pre-war models and marketed them as BMWs. These are 321s, on the assembly line, in the late 1940s.

EMW—LIKE BMW? THE SAME BUT DIFFERENT

So, what happened after the Russians expropriated the Eisenach factory, and eventually started building an automobile that they badged as the EMW? This is rather a long, complex and, in some ways, sordid story.

As mentioned in the main text, after the Iron Curtain descended in 1945 BMW's Eisenach factory found itself in Eastern Germany, and real BMW automobiles were never again made there. After the Russian juggernaut marched in, a new company called Autowelo was set up to start building motorcycles, then automobiles, at Eisenach. The Russians, who were in no mood to honor patent law, decided that they might as well make little more than remanufactured BMWs (the press tools and many other facilities were still in existence, and were not about to be shipped to Munich)—and did just that, for several years. Accordingly, for quite some time, there was a rather bizarre situation in that BMWs were being produced in West Germany, and so-called BMWs were still being built in East Germany—even if the rightful owners of the brand had nothing to do with them. Despite BMW's protests, the Russians said that this was fine as far as they were concerned—and in spite of everything, they exported many such automobiles into Western Europe.

BMW, however, persisted in their attempts to get some wrongs put right, and even though the Cold War was developing they moved a few legal mountains to unscramble a very difficult situation. By suing the dealers that distributed the counterfeit cars BMW were able to put a stop to Autowelo's attempts to market its prewar models. From that juncture, Autowelo cleverly made very minimum alterations, the automobiles they continued to produce were re-badged as EMW (Eisenacher Motoren Werke), and the BMW badge was re-touched in red-and-white.

Although no attempt seems to have been made to modernize the design of these 327-based and 340-based automobiles, no fewer than 19,000 of all such types were exported before the marque was killed off in 1956. The Russians seemed to have no expertise, nor any desire, to produce new EMW models, so the last of these automobiles was really no more advanced than the late-1930s models had ever been.

This was the line up of what was built between 1945 and 1955:

1945–50	BMW 321	8,996 automobiles
1946–47	BMW 326	16 automobiles
1952–55	BMW 327/EMW 327	505 automobiles
1949–55	BMW 340/EMW 340	21,083 automobiles

So, what happened next? It sticks in the throat of any true BMW enthusiast to point out that the authorities then got their way: to produce a "people's automobile" after all. Alongside the ageing, but still patrician, 340-based EMWs, a horrid little two-stroke 894cc-engined machine named the IFA had been developed (the Russians had also absorbed the old Audi/DKW plant at nearby Zwickau). This was then supplanted by the rather awful two-stroke-engined, front-wheel-drive Wartburg. Wartburg? Wasn't that the brand that had been a progenitor of BMW, way back in the 1890s? Indeed it was, but except for the name there was absolutely no connection between the new and the old. The historic castle, the Wartburg, remained, for after 900 years of existence this was at least as important as automobile manufacture could possibly make it. Whatever happened to the factory? The last Wartburg was built in 1991, after which that pedigree thankfully was lost. GM's Opel then bought the site, gutted and completely re-equipped it, and soon began to manufacture modern front-wheel-drive automobiles there.

OPPOSITE
Under new ownership—not that BMW would have wished it so. When the military withdrew in 1945, a Russian enterprise, Autowelo, took control of the Eisenach factory, and soon began making pre-war style BMWs once again.

kilometers from Kassel, where VWs would eventually be built in large numbers, the Iron Curtain was to be an insuperable barrier.

It took less than a year for it to become clear that the Russians wanted nothing to do with their so-called Allies in the West, were not interested in compromise of any sort, and were indifferent to any previous commercial realities. At a stroke—literally, the stroke of a pencil made on a map of Europe—BMW's Eisenach factory found itself behind the Iron Curtain, remote from BMW's influence. There it would remain for the next forty years, until German re-unification meant the end of the Iron Curtain—by which time it was far too late. Not that the Eisenach plant ceased to make automobiles. Far from it.

From 1945, the Russian Autovelo operation took over the business (naturally they never paid compensation for this), and it wasn't long before what we may describe as "counterfeit" BMWs (later badged as EMWs) were being made. This in itself was very strange, for the Russians were determined to create another "people's" paradise out of Eastern Europe, and a late-1930s BMW was by no means a "people's" automobile." From that day forward, what had once been the pride and joy of BMW's automotive empire, the factory that had done so much to establish the reputation of the brand, was lost to them for evermore, a hostage to hard-line, left-wing doctrines. Not an automobile, not an engine, nor even the tooling, or the original drawings and most of the archive of the already-legendary 300-Series automobiles, would ever again be available to the civilized West.

In the meantime, much of the original company HQ, at Milbertshofen, lay in ruins. Even before their aircraft were capable of bombing the plant, the Allies' intelligence network had identified Milbertshofen as the center of the aero-engine design, development, and testing operation, along with massive series production of the formidable Type 801 engine itself, and were therefore cold-bloodedly determined to flatten it in time. The bombers made their first attack on Munich in June 1942, causing considerably damage, Return visits were made in the following winter, and from the spring of 1943 the attacks became so intense that production had to be moved away, dispersed to a whole series of smaller, more remote, sites. This was a time when much forced labor was directed into Milbertshofen and Allach, and when motorcycle production was moved to Eisenach, to free up space to build more and more aero-engines.

When the bombing ended in 1945, and after the American Seventh Army had burst into Milbertshofen, it lay in ruins—a graphic map preserved in the BMW archive shows just how much of the factory had been razed. Although the situation was even worse in Stuttgart (where Mercedes-Benz's operation had virtually been obliterated), in Munich there was chaos all around. Half of all the buildings and half of the plant on the 3,230,000 square feet/300,000 square meter Milbertshofen site had been destroyed, and much of the rest damaged and widely dispersed. The forced labor workforce was being freed, many of the German workforce had fled, and what remained of the site looked like a wasteland. With time, money, and encouragement (all of which was lacking at that stage) it could no doubt be rebuilt, but BMW, effectively, was bust at this point. This was a shattering blow but BMW strained every sinew to make sure that the company could somehow recover. Even so, it was going to be a massive undertaking. In what was now to be known as West Germany, most BMW factories were mainly in ruins (and none of these had previously been renowned for making private automobiles), while in East Germany it was now clear that the Eisenach operation, and its satellite plants, was to be permanently out of reach.

So, was there even the makings of a business that could be rebuilt? Amazingly—though at the cost of squalor, near poverty, and much humiliation to thousands of workers, staff, and even directors—there was. Even so, it was sometimes a near thing. The occupying powers acted arrogantly, taking on the same plenipotentiary powers of old-style dictators, and simply took

away what they wanted. Allied orders originally issued from on high in July 1945 stated that BMW's entire remaining facilities were to be confiscated and shipped out as war reparations (was it legal? The Allies, it seemed, didn't care—they had won the war, after all), but in the end such edicts were slimmed down considerably. Although the Allies originally demanded that all BMW's facilities should be confiscated, but gradually a more pragmatic attitude dawned. Berlin-Spandau, on the other hand, was totally gutted and, as I have already detailed, Eisenach was taken over "for the good of the Thuringian people."

Before long, the Allach aero-engine factory was turned into a massive U.S. military vehicle repair operation, Elsewhere in Munich, BMW produced cooking utensils, building fittings,

ENGINE AFTERLIFE—BRISTOL, FRAZER-NASH AND AC

Immediately after the Second World War, "Bill" Aldington, whose British AFN company had imported BMWs during the 1930s, "liberated" some 328 engines and all the surviving blueprints and documentation out of BMW. He also persuaded engineer Fritz Fiedler to join him, and brought all back to Great Britain. Aldington encouraged the Bristol Aeroplane Co. to set up an automobile-making subsidiary, persuaded them to manufacture close copies of the 328-type engine, and saw that engine developed mightily in the next ten years.

Bristol put the engine into production in Britain for their own use, while also supplying derivatives to Frazer Nash, AC, and several racecar manufacturers. The original Bristol automobile (Type 400) was launched in 1947, and BMW experts immediately saw that this was a clever amalgam of several late-1930s BMW features (the style and chassis, for instance, was very close to that of the 327). Several hundreds were sold and other models, such as the Type 401, 403, 404, 405, and 406, soon succeeded it. The company survived by selling small numbers of very expensive machines.

Although it is believed that no fees, royalties or recompense was ever made, this gallant old BMW engine family powered every single Bristol model until it was finally dropped in favor of big Chrysler V8 power units in the early 1960s.

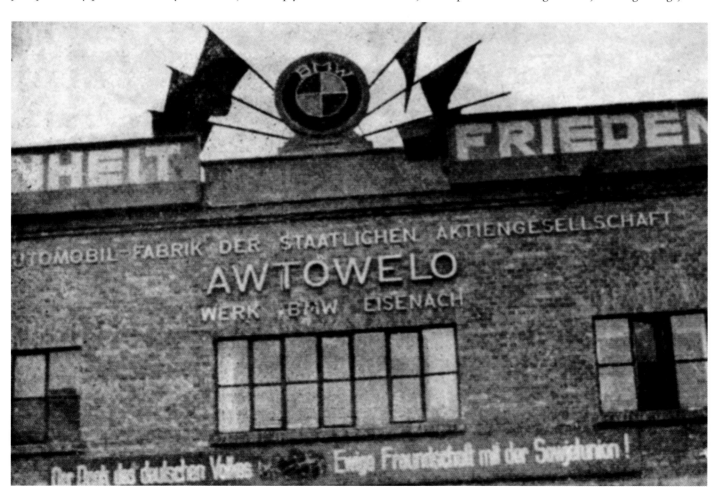

In the lean years after the Second World War, it was BMW's motorcycles which provided a boost to the company's fortunes. The real, beating, heart of the famous R 68 model was the 35bhp 600cc flat-twin engine. BMW's bikes were sought after in the higher price, more specialist market.

case, not merely because it was less heavily damaged, but because work was still proceeding on BMW's new jet engine project, which was thought to have great potential.

A return to motorcycle and automobile manufacturing

Somehow or other, BMW convinced the American authorities that they should start building motorcycles again (the motorcycle operation had originally been based in Munich, though it had been relocated to Eisenach during the war). A successor to the pre-war R23 model was produced, the R24, which was shown at the Geneva Salon in 1948—and immediately attracted several thousand orders. Although it was only a 250cc, single-cylinder, machine, it was engineered to BMW's usual standards, and soon went on sale: more than 17,000 R24s were sold in the first two years.

That was the good news. The bad news was that for ages BMW simply had no idea how they could break back into making automobiles again. Every vestige of their pre-war automotive company was now locked behind the Iron Curtain, and BMW had no way of starting up again using duplicate facilities. All documents referring to the 328 had been swept off to Britain (see the panel on page 59), and not a single complete new BMW model of any type remained at Milbertshofen. Though BMW arch-enthusiasts, such as Ernst Loof and Alex von Falkenhausen, set up their own post-war operations (Veritas and AFM respectively), to build up automobiles around reconditioned BMW 328 material, the BMW business itself struggled to stay alive.

By the end of 1949, 2,500 people were back working at Milbertshofen, building motorcycles (this compared with 6,500 who were working at Allach on non-automotive projects). However, although the two-wheeler business was once again thriving, there was still no sign of a new BMW automobile— even though, amazingly, in 1949 a tiny new automobile, the 531 project designed by Dr. Fiedler (who had returned from Britain), progressed as far as a prototype being made. It was powered by a 20bhp/600cc air-cooled motorcycle engine, and had a style rather resembling a late-1930s BMW that had been severely shrunk in the wash, but nothing came of it. Much more promising, however, was the fact that a prototype of the still-born (Eisenach-developed) 2-liter BMW 332 had been discovered, severely battered, but otherwise complete, under a pile of rubble at Milbertshofen. Not only did the resourceful engineers get this automobile going once again, but they then

bicycles, baking equipment, and agricultural machine. By late 1948 motorcycles were once again in production—but still there were no automobiles. As far as automobile enthusiasts were concerned, it all took ages for BMW to get back on to their feet. First of all, what remained of the factory had to be made weather-proof, then the Allied occupation forces had to be dissuaded from imposing a complete strip out of the facilities, and next some sort of workforce had to be re-assembled, and put to work. Allach got much of the priority at this stage in any measured it and re-measured it, from end to end, in great detail, so that a set of engineering drawings could be made, and automobiles could be made once again if needed.

And they were needed. By 1950 the German economy was somehow dragging itself back from the edge of complete disintegration, several other car-makers had begun to make private transport again—and BMW thought it could do the same. Even so, it would not be until 1951 that the first genuine post-war BMW model—the 501 (or "Baroque Angel" as it was immediately nick-named), which was an evolution of the 332—was put on show, and even then it was not yet ready for sale.

At a time when Germany was still war-torn, and struggling to get back on its feet, if any of the population was actually still in the market for transport, they really needed small automobiles (VW Beetles, for instance, were a perfect example), and not the luxurious machines that BMW had been so used to making at Eisenach in the 1930s. Not that this mattered, for BMW really had no alternative: those who had managed to re-settle in the West only knew how to make big automobiles. In any case, they reasoned, there must still be a demand for a bigger automobile; only Mercedes-Benz was providing any rivalry, and the risk was worth taking. So, it was not that what remained of BMW had some sort of death wish, nor that it was plunged into a deep pool of apathy—this was what they could do, and they thought it was worth doing it!

Not only was the "Baroque Angel" big, bulbous, and derived from the Type 332 prototype of 1941, but from 1954 it was given an all-new V8 engine (the first post-war German V8, incidentally) and called the 502. If it had been difficult to sell the expensive 501, then selling the more costly 502 would be even more demanding. To sell any numbers of the coach-built 503 and 507 types that followed was a real achievement—and losses on the automotive side continued to build up. However, at least the company once again had a toe-hold in the automotive market and, with its motorcycles continuing to sell well, the business could, rather precariously, stay afloat.

In 1945, what remained of BMW, after the bombing, was in a mess. It would need to be completely recreated to produce anything in future years.

CHAPTER 6

BAROQUE ANGELS AND BUBBLE CARS

T ENTATIVELY, BUT IN A TYPICALLY DETERMINED MANNER, BMW set about rebuilding their business in the late 1940s, but this had to be done in the teeth of opposition from the American occupation authorities. First of all the Milbertshofen factory itself had to be rebuilt. In the meantime, the partial dismantling of the plant had to be carried out (a penalty imposed for war reparations), and there was an acute shortage of manpower, such that BMW could only get up off their knees by restarting motorcycle production in 1948.

It was not until 1952 that BMW could once again begin making new-design motor cars in Munich. For manufacture in the re-built Milbertshofen plant, the 501 sedan, nicknamed "Baroque Angel", went on sale in 1952. This study shows an impressive line up of 501s, and the closely-related 502s, in the body-finishing area.

It is a measure of the devastation that the last of the rubble was not cleared away until 1947, and that dismantling did not end until mid-1949, by which time no fewer than 2,598 machines had been shipped out, and not replaced. At this point, the Allies relented, and allowed Germany to start planning for a new industrial future, by rebuilding and re-equipping its factories. A much-needed currency reform in 1948 swept away the discredited Reichsmark and replaced it with the Deutschmark. The first new production machines were installed at Milbertshofen in 1949, and a return to automobile production could begin. But not, as I have already made clear, at Eisenach. For the foreseeable future, all BMW-badged automobiles and motorcycles would have to be assembled at Milbertshofen, and although a lot of rebuilding progress had been made, yet more work would be needed to make the plant suitable for building automobiles.

The rise of the Baroque Angel

Since BMW already had the single re-born 332 as the basis of a new machine, this was to be the first post-war machine. Amazingly, BMW also discovered some pre-war 2-liter engine casting molds close to Munich, which at least gave the team a flying start. Three prototype bodies were completed, and compared—a coupe from Autenrieth of Darmstadt, a sedan shell from Farina in Italy, and a four-door sedan from BMW. The company eventually chose its own design for what became the 501: almost immediately it gained the nickname of "Baroque Angel." The launch in 1951 was premature, for the first automobiles were not delivered until late 1952, one full year after they had first been shown. More than 900,000 square feet/84,000 square meters of the rebuilt Milbertshofen site was allocated to assembly (rebuilt after the bombing, most of this was on the south of the site, close to the main administrative

BMW's very first post-war car, the 501, was previewed in 1951, and the first cars were delivered from Munich in 1952.

The first BMW production cars to be built in Munich were the 501 "Baroque Angel" series.

Ready to be painted, trimmed, then mated with the chassis frame, this 501-type body shell has just completed welding and assembly in 1955.

HQ). However, the first deliveries were made only because Baur (of Stuttgart) supplied the 1,870 body shells, while the steel body pressing and assembly facilities were being installed at Munich.

Here was a very bravely-designed new automobile, with a sturdy chassis frame, whose descendants would survive to the last 3200CS of 1965. It was the very first BMW to have a steering column gearshift. To use a descriptive German word, gemutlich (which translates as "pleasant and comfortable"), this was an automobile with plenty of space, comfortable seating, high-grade equipment, and a soft ride. Since the BMW 502 was, frankly, rather a stodgy automobile, it was heartening that three fine sporty versions—503, 507, and 3200CS—would eventually appear. Because this was a big, heavy, and—above all—costly new automobile, it could not fill the assembly halls at

Milbertshofen. Although 3,471 automobiles were produced in 1954, this compared badly with 29,699 BMW motorcycles. By 1956, 501 production had fallen to just 1080 automobiles, in 1957 it was only 611, and it dribbled to a close soon after that.

Nothing daunted, the engineers then developed a totally new 90-degree aluminum V8 engine, which was going to restore their automobiles to the top of the performance league. There was ample space within Milbertshofen's halls to install new machinery. With sporty styling likely to follow, maybe a return to motor sport was no longer out of the question? Several derivatives of this chassis/family followed. The first V8-engined model was the 502 of 1954; only a year later the 3.2 model was unveiled and its "Super" derivative had no less than 140bhp. The 502 became the BMW 2600 in 1961, the 3.2 becoming the

3200 at the same time.

In the meantime, North American importer Max Hoffman urged BMW to produce more sporty automobiles. Hoffman was not happy with BMW's own ideas, and sought artistic advice from New York resident Count Albrecht Goertz. Hoffman's patronage helped to inspire three different sporty BMWs—a 503 Coupe, a 503 Cabriolet, and a short-wheelbase 507 Roadster. Although none of these automobiles sold in big numbers, and they certainly did not contribute any profits to the company, they did at least raise the company profile when it most needed it.

Based on the same rolling chassis as the 502, the new 503 had a 140bhp 3,168cc version of the V8 engine, and there were two closely-related but intriguingly different two-door body styles. All were assembled at Milbertshofen, where they got their own dedicated assembly lines. Here, at least, were automobiles

worthy of their looks—but they were expensive. 503 and 507 models had bodies made, almost by hand, in Munich, though in the last of the line—the new 3200CS model which appeared in 1961—bodies came from Bertone of Turin, Italy, who trucked them over the Alps at a rate that never exceeded five automobiles a week.

The vast halls at Milbertshofen, though, were always under-used (the company admitted that they had to lay off workers because the 500 luxury car was not selling as well as hoped), and BMW needed another model to fill them up. Even in recent years company archivists admitted, freely, that BMW was so cash-strapped that it could not even contemplate designing, tooling, and re-equipping the assembly lines without "selling off the family silver." It was for this reason that most of the Allach aero-engine factory was sold off, to MAN, the builder of trucks, in 1960 and 1965.

BELOW
Signs of real progress at Milbertshofen came when the company could install series of massive press tool to manufacture panels for the 501 sedan—this being for the heavily contoured front fenders.

ABOVE
By the mid-1950s, and determined to turn BMW into a leading motor industry colossus, the company was installing huge clearing presses at Milbersthofen, like this 1200-ton monster.

LEFT
BMW built up their own body shells for the 501 family in the 1950s and 1960s. Nearly 23,000 would be sold before production finally ended in 1963.

FAR LEFT
As re-developed for use in the 501-family of cars, the famous BMW six-cylinder engine, whose design roots were in the 1930s, was a reliable and robust unit. This particular cylinder block is having checks carried out on the finish of the cylinder walls.

Even after the 501 was safely put into production, BMW still carried out much testing, and modification.

Making the "bubble car"

Accordingly, this explains why it was a cuter, though ludicrously under-powered "bubble car"—the Isetta—that allowed BMW to turn the corner. An Italian concern, Iso, introduced the Isetta, which had a front-opening door and an air-cooled two-stroke engine on the right side, behind the seats. BMW engineer Eberhard Wolff saw this automobile at the Geneva Motor Show and alerted his bosses to its potential. Although it was totally different from the Baroque Angel, there were compensations. Iso offered to conclude a building agreement, but would also sell their own body presses for BMW to build the machines in numbers. BMW, for their own part, chose to fit their own BMW R25 type 12bhp/245cc four-stroke motorcycle engine. Originally on sale from April 1955 (it cost 2,550DM/about $600) the Isetta was a success (12,911 units were delivered in the first full year), and it would sell for the

next eight years, latterly with a larger (15bhp/298cc) engine, and a restyled cabin. For some markets, with favorable tax structures, it was built with only a single rear wheel.

Although BMW was only precariously in profit (though not nearly as money-making as they would become in the 1970s and beyond), the Milbertshofen plant was still simply equipped. Production, however, soared after the "bubble" phenomenon took root. The first fifty 501s had been built in 1952, 3,770 were produced in 1954, but by 1958 no fewer than 50,256 automobiles of all types were completed. This was a relief, as motorcycle sales had peaked in 1954, but had then slumped to a mere 5,400 in 1957.

Although the little Isetta didn't earn much, it kept the workforce in place, but it did nothing for the company's previous up-market image. Business, though, was business, and the company then developed this "building block" further by

OPPOSITE
Full, yes. Busy, yes—but not yet over-crowded. This was the body shop at Milbersthofen, in 1955, when the Baroque Angel's popularity was at its height.

In the mid-1950s BMW reacted strongly to the boom in small-car sales, and began making the tiny motorcycle-engined Isetta bubble car. Here, in 1956, a new Isetta is almost complete, needing only a seat and a rear parcel shelf to be fitted.

Installations set up to deal with the bulky 501 range of BMWs could easily swallow the thousands of Isetta bubble cars which joined them in the assembly halls at Milbertshofen. These bodies are in the middle of the painting process.

By 1960, most traces of the original BMW factory in Munich had been swept away, and new buildings had been erected in their place. The 501 gives an idea of the scale of the Munich plant building number 11 which dates from 1916.

designing an altogether larger and less graceful four-seater automobile that it called the 600. The 600 was much more than a stretched Isetta, for the engine was now mounted in the absolute tail, and this was the company's first, and only, four-seater "bubble" car. Strangely enough, access to the front seats was still by a forward-opening clamshell door (as with the Isetta, the steering wheel/column folded upwards and forwards as the door was opened), with rear-seat access by a conventional door in the right side (kerb side, on European and North American roads) of the body shell. Inescapably, the 600 was more costly, at 3,985 DM (about $900) it was close to the price of a good second-hand VW Beetle.

In three years, BMW sold no fewer than 34,813 600s, all of which were produced at Milbertshofen, and used air-cooled flat-twin BMW-type motorcycle engines that were machined and assembled close by in another factory building. Looking back, though, the 600 was not an automobile (should I even write "automobile"?) that really appealed to BMW's board of directors, nor (not for long, anyway) the buying public.

Technically it fell between every possible stool—too large to be a bubble, too small for a "real automobile," and mechanically still too crude to fight it out with other major rivals. However, as far as company accountants were concerned, it kept the production lines respectably busy during that time. The same rebuilt assembly halls that produced 501s, 502s and their closely related models (including the gorgeous 507 two-seater), went on to build many more Isettas and 600s—maybe the workforce was not proud of what they were screwing together, but it all helped to put food on the table.

The 700: a modern post-war automobile

The real marketing breakthrough followed in 1959, when BMW introduced what was arguably their first modern, truly post-war, automobile: the sharply-styled 700. If the company's finances had still not been in such a state, the 700 might have reached the market earlier: the miracle was that it appeared at all. BMW had finally swallowed their pride, and hired an independent styling consultant, an amazingly productive little Italian called Giovanni Michelotti. Born in Turin, and originally working for Farina (in 1937), Michelotti had run his own business since 1949. By the 1950s he had produced several noted styles (some of them being sexy one-offs on Ferraris), and was already famous. Even so, it was not until 1958 that he was contracted to refine a new style that the Austrian BMW importer, Wolfgang Denzel (who also made his own-brand of sports cars) had proposed.

The result was the birth of the BMW 700, which was a total change in BMW's image: here was a range of compact automobiles with a smart, sharp-edged, style. As opposed to the dumpy 600, the 700 looked like a real automobile (though it retained a motorcycle type engine), and it was something of which BMW could once again be proud. It was totally different from anything previously seen behind the BMW badge. Although there were technical links between the old and the new—the flat-twin air-cooled engine and the front and rear suspensions were obviously related—this was the very first BMW to have a pressed-steel unit-construction body/chassis shell. Clearly this cost a great deal of scarce investment capital—and as BMW was back in a loss-making situation, there were problems.

Time for modernization

By this time, frankly, BMW's facilities at Milbertshofen were beginning to look antiquated. There was still too much "sticking plaster" of rebuilding and modernization around the plant, and much of the plant had been purchased in the United States back in 1949. The remains of the old oval test track were still in evidence, but no longer used, and there were unused huts, sheds, and small buildings. Not only that, but even by late 1950's standards—when the building of automobiles was much simpler than it became fifty years later—the way that BMW automobiles were built was still a very simple process. Body shells were welded together by hand-operated spot-pincers, the paint shop was so primitive that the guns were directed by hand, the treatment of waste was also basic in the extreme, while pollution and noise levels were high. Each factory block seemed to have its own individual heating system (usually fired by oil, but occasionally by coal).

The cost of modernizing the plant (the need for which was well recognized by the Board, who were almost powerless to take action) was a major factor behind BMW's financial crisis, which came to a head in December 1959. Lumber magnate Hermann Krages had already invested heavily in the company,

but he resigned before the 700 could be launched, and even a proposed loan from the Bavarian government was not enough. This all precipitated the traumatic events that so nearly led to BMW being absorbed by Daimler-Benz, which are covered in the next chapter.

Although automobile buffs might now stifle a yawn, the sequence of events is important. BMW knew that it was running out of money, and was reluctant to launch new automobiles, yet the original 700 Coupe was launched in August 1959, the financial crisis meeting followed in December 1959, and the 700 sedan appeared immediately after that. This under-financed gamble soon paid off, for BMW built 42,524 automobiles in 1959, would lift that to 53,729 in 1960, and all the trends finally looked to be upwards.

The new 700 range not only had a very rigid unit-body structure, but for the very first time the planners had laid out a range of automobiles, logically and at minimum cost. There were three different two-door body styles, two wheelbase lengths, and two different power outputs. It wasn't long before the 700 became BMW's best-selling automobile so far—56,000 Sedans would be built in three years, and the 600 was soon killed off.

In the hiatus which followed the traumas of 1959 this all proved to be highly profitable, and Milbertshofen boomed as never before. There's no question that the 700 range did a great job for BMW, cleverly bridging the gap between the Isettas, 600s, and "Baroque Angels" of the 1950s, and the unstoppable growth of the New Generation sedans of the 1960s. It was the 700s that held the line for BMW until the New Class 1500s, 1800s, and 2000s could make their own reputation in the 1960s—in fact they were only withdrawn when the factories became crammed with the larger, faster, and more profitable machines. BMW's huge growth was just about to begin, as these statistics make clear.

For the first time since 1945, BMW could start to boast about production figures—and they duly did so. In six years, no fewer than 188,121 700-family machines were built, of which 36,761 were coupes of one length or another, but only 2,592 were of the more expensive little Cabriolets. And did Giovanni Michelotti get his reward? Indeed he did, for no sooner had the 700s been adopted than he also become involved in the shaping of the new 1500 sedan: he would become one of BMW's most favored consultants in the years that followed.

All, however, was not sweetness and light at BMW, for this was the period when the company so nearly lost its independence.

CHAPTER 7

FIGHTING OFF PREDATORS—AND LAUNCHING THE "NEW CLASS"

B Y THE LATE 1950S, THE ISETTA BUBBLE CARS and the 600 range had bought BMW one precious commodity: time. As the 501 generation had continued to lose money with almost every example that rolled out of the door, the tiny down-market air-cooled automobiles not only provided more sales, but kept the workforce fully employed.

Even so, it wasn't enough, and even schoolboy economists could see why. In marketing terms there was a colossal gap in the BMW range between the tiny bubble-based automobiles, and the massive, overblown, 500-series machines. That gap did not persist because of ignorance, but because of a lack of money. BMW's management knew that the Milbertshofen factory was still under-used—space was never a problem at this stage, especially as at least two or more bubble cars could be built in the space taken up by one 500-series machine—but modern automobiles were missing. What they really wanted to do was to fill that gap—first of all by building the Michelotti-styled 700s (this was, at least, financially possible, and was achieved), but then they wanted to follow it up with an all-new medium-sized machine (this became the "New Class" that would become the original 1500)—but the investment capital was simply not available to make this possible.

A "New Class" model in preparation on the final assembly line at the Munich factory in 1964. It is probably an 1800 model and behind it on the line are BMW 700s which remained in production until 1965.

Dealing with Daimler-Benz

To put the "New Class" on sale, BMW would have to design the automobile themselves, and would not only have to invest in new body shell press tooling and assembly facilities, but in everything needed to build a modern engine in large quantities. Although the engineers were already working on new-generation 4-cylinder engines, complete with overhead-camshaft valve gear, and the possibility of evolving a straight-6-cylinder engine from the same design roots as the "four," entirely new machine tools and flow-line assembly installations would be needed. Major decisions would have to be made, and soon, for at a time when plenty of capital was needed to install new facilities, the company's finances were still in an awful state. It could be argued, and rightly so, that the company had never really recovered from the Second World War (especially as they had lost the use of Eisenach). By late 1959, the situation was so bad that the local (Bavarian) government became thoroughly alarmed at the potential loss of jobs in Munich, for they also concluded that motorcycles, and bubble cars, were not likely to keep BMW afloat. They offered to invest heavily in the business to help keep it alive, mainly to support Allach's continuing work on aero-engines.

Even so, this was never likely to be enough to help launch a new automobile, so further financial investment was still needed. As a German historian later commented, when surveying BMW's development in this period: "Around this time, rumors of a merger or takeover involving a German or foreign company were heard often. From America and England, so it went, potential buyers or investors were visiting Munich in rapid succession. True enough, there were signs of interest, but serious negotiations never took place. BMW's management still believed, as incredible as it may seem, that it would be able to pull the company up by its own bootstraps…"

The crunch came in December 1959. This was the period in which BMW's directors proposed to write down (diminish the value of) the existing shares by 50 percent, and would then issue new shares, which would only to be available to participating banks—and to Daimler-Benz of Stuttgart! So, once again, the specter of BMW being overshadowed by a larger, and bitter, rival, raised itself. We must not forget that the first links with Daimler-Benz had come in the 1920s (some directors having shareholdings and influence inside both companies), and that even in the dark days of Nazi Germany the two companies had co-operated (at least to the extent of staying off each other's aero-engine patch!).

Financially, philosophically, and—somehow—in terms of

ABOVE
In the early 1960s, Munich's factory was busily occupied by manufacturing rear-engined 700s, either sedans or coupes. This was the first real BMW after the war and the dealers persuaded the stockholders to reject the sale to Daimler Benz on the strength of the expected sales of this model.

OPPOSITE:
Announced in 1959, the 700 range was a successful attempt to build up sales at a difficult time. By 1962, when this study was taken, the 700 was still the most numerous car in the Milbertshofen factory, with annual production of all BMWs now in excess of 50,000 units.

Workers assembling the "New Class" BMW 1500 on the production line in the early 1960s.

new name—that of multi-millionaire Herbert Quandt—came to light, as he took a major shareholding. From that day to this, the Quandts have held a position of real influence in BMW, and have made sure that they retained their independence. Along with this backing, and (most importantly) that of the major banks, the fortunes of the company gradually—very gradually— began to turn around. Amazingly, it soon began to look as if BMW would still survive.

The New Class

Survival meant injecting new blood into the model range and the concept of the "New Class" became a very important part of the product mix. Significantly, because money was still short, BMW did not introduce a complete range of new styles, but just one new type—a four-door sedan. It would be many years before the company could afford to invest by extending the range to include convertibles (traditionally manufactured for them by quality coachbuilders Karosserie Baur of Stuttgart) and wagons (the Touring Range as it is known in BMW parlance). Years too, in the future, before they ventured back into two-seater sports cars.

Not only that, but there was no question of erecting a totally new assembly plant in which to produce the automobiles. When it was ready, the "New Class" model would have to be manufactured in the Milbertshofen plant, and to do this the older models would have to be swept aside. From 1959 to 1963, visitors to the plant would see that steady, methodical, change brought massive improvements to the facilities, and a roll call of comings and goings proved a point:

real-world sentiment, this deal never felt right. All the signs were that, if it went through, BMW would soon become a minor partner in the combine, that they would spend much time supplying parts to Daimler-Benz for Mercedes-Benz automobiles, and that the BMW brand might soon vanish altogether. The tide of disapproval was immediate—and strident. Everyone, except BMW's board and Daimler-Benz, objected to the proposal, and a group of small stockholders demanded further discussion. When the directors decided to put the matter to an Extraordinary General Meeting of shareholders in December 1959, this meeting went on for a tumultuous nine hours before being adjourned with the Daimler-Benz offer still not approved.

The offer was finally thrown out, instigating a cataclysm that caused Chairman Dr. Richter-Brohm (who had only been in a position of real power since 1955) to resign. As a result, the proposals were much diluted, the existing capital was written down by only 25 percent, and this was the point, too, at which a

1958	Final production of 6-cylinder 500-series automobiles
1959	Final production of 600 models
1962	Final production of Isetta bubble cars
August 1962	Start-up of series-production 1500 "New Class" sedans
1965	Final production of BMW-bodied V8-cylinder 500-series automobiles
1965	Final production of 700-series automobiles

By 1963, in other words, the "New Class" sedan was taking over as the dominant model at Milbertshofen, and by that time, in any case, the last of the V8-engined automobiles (the Bertone-bodied 3200CS coupe) and the 700 series automobiles were under sentence of death.

A turnaround in company fortunes

This, then, was just the start of the transformation that changed BMW from the builders of quirky and none-too-modern automobiles at Milbertshofen—without filling that factory, or without making profits in the process—to a company which built an ever-increasing number of "New Class" automobiles. This was followed up by launching a sports coupe version of the machine, then the first of the "02" models, and finally taking a very brave pill and introducing the original 6-cylinder 2500/2800 range of sedans in 1968. To do this, the company took advantage of profits that were finally beginning to flood in,

along with the positive cash flow that resulted from it. Sales would increase, steadily—yet many do not realize that the company did not build more than 100,000 automobiles in a year until 1968, and even this figure was only achieved after Hans Glas GmbH had been acquired in 1966.

Even so, at Milbertshofen alone, BMW invested 1.1 billion Deutschmarks (approximately $300 million) in factory improvements in the ten years starting with the installation of new facilities for the "New Class" in the early 1960s. One of the most important individual projects was to build what was known as "Building 140," which was to be devoted to the

One of the 1960s generation of new BMWs, which quite changed the company's prospects, goes into one of the paint booths in Munich.

OPPOSITE
At the end of the 1950s, BMW knew that it needed to introduce a range of all-new medium-sized cars—like these 1500s, which soon followed—but they lacked the financial resources to carry that out. It was only after a traumatic period, when the financially-frail BMW might once have been absorbed by Daimler-Benz, that the Quandt family agreed to inject a great deal of capital to save the operation.

production of mechanical items, and engine assembly: four years later an addition (Building 140.1) was completed. These were erected on the site of the old oval running-in/test track, which had also included aero-engine test beds.

All this was brave investment, for although the 1500 "New Class" was certainly that—new from end to end, smart, crisply styled, and technologically advanced—it took some time for the German public to accept it. Looking back, though, one wonders why? Not only was it a smart looker, but the overhead-camshaft engine that the noted engineer Alex von Falkenhausen had produced was not only as modern as any other in Germany, but at the very beginning of its development cycle, and there was also a very effective semi-trailing arm independent rear suspension. By this period in history, however, it began to look as if fortune was at last shining down on BMW. Soon after the "New Class" automobiles first appeared, one of Germany's long-established automobile-making companies, Borgward, collapsed and could not be revived. The good news for BMW was that Borgward's Isabella range included a popular 1.5-liter range of middle-class sedans that the 1500 could replace at once, if only the public would recognize this.

BMW's new management, now securely and generously backed by Herbert Quandt (who wanted to see a return on his investment!) was confident that the turn-around would eventually happen—and it did. Slowly, and as it turned out, permanently, buyers in the marketplace turned towards BMW for their new middle-class automobiles. Not only had BMW produced a fine new automobile, but for the first time since 1939 the company seemed to have a coherent range of products, starting with the last of the Isettas, moving up through the still smart 700 range, going on to the new and exciting 1500, all topped out by the very last of the "Baroque Angel" based machines. To this one could add the motorcycles, which had recovered much of their reputation.

For the first time in years, there was no immediate financial

crisis to distract the managers, who could carry on developing this strategy. By recognizing that the "New Class" could be not one, but a whole series of automobiles, the sales force could eventually offer several different models, and even change the front and rear end styles to suit. Sales continued to edged upwards—they passed 60,000 for the first time in 1964, and would reach 88,000 only three years later. Not only that, but the company had settled on a coherent engineering theme—in future the structures would feature unit-construction body shells, engines would all be based on the new overhead-camshaft layout, suspension would be all-independent (with that characteristic semi-trailing layout at the rear)—and each type would demonstrably be related to another. This was also a period in which the product mix changed quite radically. The last Isetta was produced in 1962, the very last of the "Baroque Angel" generation of sedans (the 2600/3200 types) was built in 1963, and the last of the cute rear-engined 700 range followed in 1965. On the other hand, the 1500 grew up, becoming an 1800 in 1963, and a developed 1600 in 1964, while a smart coupe derivative was added in 1965. And there was more to follow.

All of this was achieved within the same ground space that Milbertshofen had always offered, though by the mid-1960s the area had become almost entirely developed. Successively-published aerial views show old buildings demolished and new ones erected, but always within the constraints of the four public roads that surrounded the site. By the 1960s, certainly, few of the original buildings that progressively filled the estate in the 1930s still remained.

In only a few years, of course, the atmosphere within BMW had changed completely. Before the 1960s opened, the fear had always been that the business might collapse completely. By the end of the decade, however, the Milbertshofen site was completely developed, and could expand no further. It was time for the next big leap forward—and that opportunity came close by, at Dingolfing, when the company took over Glas.

By 1958 the Milbertshofen plant in Munich was rapidly running out of ground where new buildings could be installed. The remains of the motorcycle test track (soon to disappear) can still be seen.

Could BMW have survived the turbulent 1950s and early 1960s without making ultra-small cars? There's no question that the building of tens of thousands of 700s helped them finance the bigger and more glamorous cars which were to follow. This is how 700 Coupe shells were transported, in bulk, to the SKD Moorhens assembly plant in Belgium, for completion in 1964.

THE BIG LEAP FORWARD

CHAPTER 8

BUYING UP GLAS, BUILDING UP THE BUSINESS

BY THE LATE 1960S, BMW'S ANNUAL AUTOMOBILE SALES were pushing up towards the 100,000 mark. If not then, but soon, it seemed clear that the existing Milbertshofen plant would soon be completely developed, and incapable of further physical expansion. All signs of war-time damage had been eliminated many years before, every possible square foot of the existing ground was either built over, or concrete plans were already in place to do so—yet BMW's bosses were looking for further expansion.

The best-selling "02" range was launched at Munich in 1966. Rarest of all, and seen only briefly in 1973 and 1974, was this derivative, the turbocharged 2002 Turbo, easily recognised by the wheel-arch extensions and the big front spoiler.

When BMW celebrated their fiftieth anniversary—in 1966, exactly half a century after the original aircraft-engine building business had been founded—the company's top men already knew that they were facing up to major challenges. The bad old hand-to-mouth days of ten years earlier had gone, the company was clear of unwanted debt—and it was anxious to find more space, so that more automobiles could be produced. This was made all the more imperative by the launch of the company's new type of two-door family sedans—first of all the 1600–2, with the 1802, the 2002, and other derivatives of the same automobile to follow.

In September 1961, the first of the "New Class" 1500s had been one of the undoubted stars of the Frankfurt Motor Show, though it took a full year to get the early production automobiles into the showrooms. If only we had known it, not only was this a new beginning for the Bavarian company but their layout set a template for generations of new models that were to follow. Take one look at these basic features, and their developments, or descendants, may still be recognized in BMWs of the early 2000s. The 1,499cc engine was a sturdy 4-cylinder unit with overhead camshaft valve gear, all installed at a 30

degree angle towards the right side (kerb side, as it was to be in most European countries, and the United States) of the engine bay. Independent front suspension was by MacPherson struts, independent rear suspension was by coil springs, and front-wheel disc brakes were standard. Prototypes were advertised with 75bhp, but production automobiles all had 80bhp, and the claimed top speed was 92mph/148kph. The first quoted price was 8,500 DM/$2,125.

The initial style, an evolution of shapes commissioned by Michelotti, was of a roomy four-door five-seater sedan monocoque, with a forward-leaning nose (no-one seemed to worry about low drag coefficients in those days), a stylized version of the famous BMW "kidney" grille, and of course with the blue-and-white BMW badge immediately above it. It was not just this automobile but the implication of what would follow that was so important to BMW. They already knew (though the public was not yet told) that one day the 4-cylinder engine could be stretched all the way to 2.0-liters—they also knew that 6-cylinder versions could be developed, and that those could eventually be pushed right out to 3.3-liters.

Nor was BMW so shortsighted as to try to make every mechanical item in its automobiles. There were limits—financial and spatial—to what could be achieved. Body shells were stamped, welded together and painted at Milbertshofen, while castings for engines and back axles came from the foundry, and were later machined and manufactured. In due course, when BMW production had expanded further, the company's manual transmissions would all be supplied by Getrag, and automatic transmissions would come from ZF.

Production pressures build

Well before it went on sale, the demand for the "New Class" automobiles built up rapidly—even in mid 1962, and with the automobile still not on sale, BMW claimed that 20,000 customers had placed orders. Facilities laid down at Milbertshofen—which could produce up to fifty automobiles a day (that many automobiles are built there in an hour these days!)—clearly could not cope, so once the money was there every effort was made to re-jig the existing site, to add more shifts, and to squeeze more capacity out of every building in the complex that BMW staff called "Werke 1." By 1963 the 1500 was in full production, and production pressures were obvious. Since more derivatives of the "New Class" were due for launch in the next two years, one by one the old, marginal-selling automobiles had to be dropped. First of all it was the Isetta

GLAS—HAD YOU EVER HEARD OF THEM?

Until Hans Glas GmbH started producing the Goggomobil mini-automobile in 1954/55, the motoring world knew next to nothing about the company. Like post-1945 BMW, Glas was based in Bavaria. Way back, in the 1880s, this family enterprise had set up shop at Pilsting an der Isar (later re-named Dingolfing), and was a modest little concern that had manufactured agricultural machinery for many years. Then, as the German nation began to recover from the utter devastation of the Second World War, something of an "economic miracle" developed. Glas spied an opening for a new type of people's transport, and launched the new Goggo motor scooter in 1951, following it up with the original two-stroke Goggomobil automobile, which was launched at the end of 1954. Although Glas proposed to build this cute little 247cc/air-cooled/rear-engined automobile in a brand-new plant at Dingolfing, about 65 miles (100 kilometers) northeast of Munich, BMW treated it with disdain at first. This, maybe, was not wise, for 9,000 were sold in the first year, and in the end more than 280,000 would be completed—which made it real competition for the existing small BMWs.

BMW was not really interested in Glas until that company's finances crumbled and a useful business became available for very little new capital. However, the company expanded and improved its product range quite remarkably in only ten years. What we might call "real automobiles" followed in 1962: the 1004 was a machine graced by a overhead-camshaft engine, and within two years there were bigger, sleeker and faster models that began to rival BMW—if not in build quality and world-wide reputation, then most certainly in performance. Not for nothing was a Ghia-styled 2600 V8 Coupe nicknamed a "Glaserati."

When BMW took over the business it was mainly interested in expanding the existing (though hopelessly out-moded) Glas factory for its own purposes, rather than developing new Glas automobiles. Although a series of new automobiles was announced in the later 1960s, this was only a holding operation and the last Glas-badged automobiles of all were produced in 1968. For this marque it had been a short and eventful life, of just fourteen years, but without it BMW might not have been able to expand so sturdily, at the time, as it did.

bubble car that got the chop, then the last of the Baroque Angels, and then the 700 models. The Bertone 3200 CS coupe, which sold only 200 automobiles a year, was squeezed into a corner and allowed to rot on the vine. By 1965, in fact, only "New Class" automobiles and motorcycles were still being made at Milbertshofen—this being a complete sea change compared with 1961.

It was during this time that the Allach factory (which had always confined itself to aero-engine production, and development) gradually faded out of this business story. Having spent some years as a massive vehicle service and repair depot for the American army fleets of vehicles, it then took on the job of building jet aero-engines for use in the reborn German military air force. Eventually this activity was hived off, and the balance of the business was sold off to MAN (then, and now, this concern built big and very capable commercial vehicles).

The 1500 was joined by the 90bhp/1800 in 1963, the 1500 itself grew up to an 83bhp/1600 in 1964, after which there was the 110bhp/1800Ti, the limited-production 1800 TI/SA "homologation special" competition sedan—and from 1965 the launch of the 2000CS coupe. The 2000/Ti/tii models—maturity at last for the "New Class"—appeared from 1966 onwards, by which time BMW's annual output was well on its way to the 100,000 mark.

Because there was absolutely no space at Milbertshofen for the manufacture of the new two-door coupe style (which was based on the platform of the 1600/1800/2000 sedan), BMW arranged for the entire shell to be completed by the independent concern Karmann, at Osnabruck in the north of West Germany,

ABOVE
Even after it had launched a series of technically advanced cars, Glas was still proud of the Goggomobils which continued to make good profits in the late 1950s. The 100,000th Goggomobil was produced in Dingolfing in 1958, but it would be eight more years before BMW bought the business, and began expanding the premises.

To boost its range in the late 1950s, Glas introduced the Isar range, cars which were larger than the Goggomobils, but would be considerably smaller than the later models which followed.

BELOW OPPOSITE
Glas already had a fine administrative building when BMW began to take an interest in the business in the early 1960s, but the factory would be rapidly expanded after the rescue and takeover of 1966.

By 1963, Glas's production range was expanding, but the Isar T600 and T700 types were the most numerous to leave Dingolfing.

and it was Karmann that also completed the automobile from components supplied from Munich. Later in the decade, when the 2000CS was directly replaced by the 2800CS, Karmann retained that contract—and would build all such BMW coupes until the mid-1970s.

Two major new model launches caused BMW to push their Milbertshofen capacity to the absolute limits in the late 1960s, and with a workforce well in excess of 10,000, they needed all the help—physical, mental and financial—that they could get. Starting in March 1966, BMW announced the first of their two-door "02" models—originally giving it the title of 1600-2—and little more than two years later they launched an all-new 6-cylinder family of automobiles, the 2500 and 2800 models. This meant that in 1968 total BMW production exceeded 100,000 for the first time, and it would then surge ahead to 161,165 in 1970.

For a company that had been a shattered wreck in 1945, and which had not built its first post-war automobiles until 1952, it was astonishing—and the fact that BMW motorcycle assembly had to be moved, completely, from Munich to Spandau, in Berlin, in 1969, tells its own story. When I quote the total production achieved by the three significant BMW model ranges of this decade, one realizes just how Milbertshofen came to be bursting at the seams:

New Class	(1962–72)	350,729
1600–2 (02 Class)	(1966–77)	759,877
2500–3.3L (Class)	(1968–77)	198,875

Within a short time, in any case, the sale of "02" class of automobiles had quite outstripped "New Class" models, for the 1600-2 was soon joined by the convertible (as bodied by Baur), the three-door hatchback 1600 Touring, the 1802, the 2002, the Cabriolet, the 2002 Ti and in due course by the limited-production 2002 turbo. The miracle is that BMW was able to produce all these automobiles, and more, without suffering a reduction in product quality.

The launch of the 6-cylinder engined automobiles—the 2500 and 2800—was a particularly brave move, which BMW could surely only contemplate because their 4-cylinder automobiles were now making so much money for them, and allowing investment capital to build up. These twins (they were virtually mechanically identical except for the use of 150bhp/2,494cc and 170bhp/2,788cc versions of the new straight 6-cylinder engine) both had to fight, head-on, against automobiles in the Mercedes-Benz range and, when they were eventually put on sale in the United States, had to measure up against Jaguar's new XJ6 models too. As always planned, these engines were effectively one-and-a-half versions of the well-liked 4-cylinder types, sharing many components, and the same basic valve gear, overhead camshaft drive, and details such as pistons, connecting rods and other details. Transmissions came from ZF, independent suspension looked the same as before—but was different in almost every detail—and these were the very first BMWs to be produced with disc brakes on all four wheels.

Because the entire body shell/monocoque of the 2500/2800 was to be pressed, welded and assembled at Milbertshofen, from this moment on it meant that for 1969 there would be three different ranges of automobiles, in a complete rainbow choice of derivatives, in production on the same site. Although a 6-cylinder coupe, the 2800CS, was launched at the same time there was absolutely no way that assembly of this automobile could be completed in-house. Because the new coupe was a successor to the 2000CS model, as before it was manufactured on BMW's behalf by Karmann, in Osnabruck, many hundreds of miles away. Karmann pressed, assembled, painted and trimmed the shells, with all the running gear being sent from Munich, or delivered direct by suppliers.

The acquisition of Glas

Even with the motorcycle facilities about to be moved to Berlin, the Milbertshofen complex was bursting at the seams, and this brave quart-in-a-pint-pot business would soon need to be relieved. At this time, therefore, the possibility of buying up a rival company, and taking over its factory with the possibility of making it much larger, came as a heaven-sent opportunity.

That chance had already appeared in 1966, when a much smaller company in Lower Bavaria—Hans Glas GmbH—had signaled its distress. Here was a small company, based at Dingolfing, about 65 miles/100km northeast of Munich, and one that was already known for its technical bravery. Unhappily its ambitions ran far ahead of its financial ability, and the business was rapidly running out of money. More than 4,000 workers were employed in what was an increasingly cramped site—a railroad line on one boundary made expansion impossible in that direction, but there were still green fields in the other direction, towards a large river. Later, a financial analysis showed that it was only Glas's quirky but distinctly non-glamorous small automobiles—particularly the Goggomobil itself (once a competitor for BMW's 700)—that were making money, whereas their smart coupes, with their advanced overhead-camshaft engines, were all sure-fire loss-makers.

Neither then, nor in future years, could BMW be accused of being aggressive towards Glas. It was a legendary one-time German motorcycle racing driver, Schorsch Meier, who acted as an "honest broker" at first, persuading each group of directors to speak to each other, and the very first fruits of this were that BMW agreed to set up a common sales organization with Glas. This, though, could really only be a temporary "finger in the dyke" operation, for what Glas needed was to bring down its costs and force up its sales. To BMW, the only real rationale of co-operation was for it to take command of Glas and, as soon as possible, to modernize, convert and dramatically expand the Dingolfing factory for its own purposes. To their eternal credit, the local authorities understood, and supported, this strategy, and made sure that extra land was made available close by. By early 1967 BMW had assumed control of the Glas business, complete with a faithful workforce of 3,700, not only at Dingolfing, but also at Landshut (which was between Dingolfing and Munich)—and already had its eyes on the transformation of the entire Dingolfing site. This was by no means the last of its expansion projects (the Steyr diesel-engine operation, and the setting up of yet more factories in Regensburg, in South Africa, in Great Britain, and in the United States would be others in future years), though this was certainly the first of what we might call the step-changes that quite transformed the face of BMW in future years. In 1966, pre-Glas acquisition, BMW produced 74,076 automobiles, while just ten years later that figure had risen to 275,022—which was a 370 percent transformation. Not only that, but forty years later Dingolfing had grown so much that it was the largest of any BMW plant worldwide, with a daily output of 1,350 automobiles.

For the moment, however, the existing Glas operation was shored up, a series of interim new Glas models was introduced (including a smart BMW 1600GT coupe, which was a re-engined Glas model), while more and more of the component work that had previously been crammed into Milbertshofen was moved into the newly-acquired plant. That, though, was only the beginning, for in 1970 the BMW board authorized the building of a brand new plant at Dingolfing, which would soon become the home of a brand-new 5-Series range, and other models after that. This was just one more in a series of expansion moves made at that time.

CHAPTER 9

MASSIVE EXPANSION—SEDANS AND SPORTS COUPES

FOR THE NEXT THREE DECADES, IT SEEMS, BMW was constantly playing catch-up—there always seemed to be more customers than automobiles that could be made. Sales continued to rise, the number of new models increased—but no sooner had factories been enlarged to cope than the whole business started again. Simple, raw statistics, tell their own story. In 1970, BMW had sold 161,000 automobiles, in 1980 that figure rose to 330,000, and by 1990 sales had ballooned yet again to 530,000. Existing factories could not cope, and even though component production was dispersed as widely as possible, new plant was still needed.

The first of BMW's modern straight-six engined cars—the 2500 and 2800 types—went into production at Munich/ Milbertshofen in 1968.

Although the need for more manufacturing space certainly applied even in the early 1970s, when the original 6-cylinder sedans were selling in such gratifying numbers, for the first time in many years BMW also found time to build a prestigious new HQ building at Milbertshofen. Because, as ever, space at Milbertshofen was at a premium, the architects built up, rather than out. BMW concluded that the new building simply had to be ready before the Olympic Games opened in the city (or at least to look ready, for the main stadium was not far away), so the HQ was erected a breakneck speed, and was visually complete by late 1972. The result was a startlingly modern twenty-two storey office block at the southern extremity of the site. Because of its unique construction, with floor after floor effectively suspended around a sturdy central core (and this will be obvious by looking at images of the building) it was immediately dubbed the "4-cylinder building." The bowl-shaped company museum building was linked to one side. The official completion date was June 1973, and more than 2,000 employees made a new home inside. Later, in the opening years of the new century, the radically new BMW Welt building would be placed on the other side of the main road, connected to both the museum and "4-cylinder" building by an overhead walkway.

Rationalization of the production facilities

But if demand continued to increase—as BMW most fervently hoped that it would—the HQ building was not about to ease the sheer congestion that now existed at Milbertshofen; 193,000 vehicles had been built there in 1973. Not only were the smaller (two-door-based) 1600–2 and the glossy new 2500/2800 6-cylinder-engined sedans dominating the production halls, but the original "New Class" family was finally phased out, to be replaced in the autumn of 1972 by the first of the new 5-Series models. Although this automobile was not all new—engines, transmissions and some suspension items were carried forward from the last of the "New Class" automobiles—the body shell was different and put a further strain on Milbertshofen's facilities.

To break the logjam, a start had already been made on reducing the number of different products that were made in Munich. Motorcycles, which had first been built in Munich during the 1920s and had been the first to be revived after the repair and rebuilding of the bomb-shattered plant in the late 1940s, were the first to be squeezed out—assembly of these was finally removed to Spandau, Berlin, where it would remain. As already noted, the Spandau plant was one of BMW's oldest

production locations. It had once built aero-engines for military aircraft (including the legendary three-engined Ju52 military transport), and had already been producing motorcycle parts since 1949 to service the build-up of motorcycle production in Munich. Once top management decided that Spandau should concentrate on complete motorcycle manufacture this became the dedicated two-wheeler plant, where up to 500 machines would be built every day by the turn of the century. Even so, there was still space for some private automobile component manufacture to take place here—brake discs, for instance, for BMW automobiles.

The big change, however, came in 1972/1973, not only because of the launch of the original 5-Series automobile, but by the completion of the first massive phase of expansion at Dingolfing. By BMW standards this was not a smooth changeover, but it was welcome nevertheless. First of all, the ten-year career of the "New Class" automobiles was brought to an end in Milbertshofen, and for the time being the 5-Series went into production on that site. As Britain's Autocar magazine analysts commented when reviewing the new 5-Series in September 1972:

"At the time of our visit in early August, the 520 was already flowing down the line at Munich. The bodies were being prepared and equipped on a line of their own, but for main mechanical assembly and final trimming they joined a common line with the 1602, 2002 and 6-cylinder sedans. BMW were hoping to have some 3,000 automobiles ready for the September launch date…"

No matter how efficient, willing and resourceful were the associates at Milbertshofen, this cannot have been an ideal situation—and it was not to last, since it was only intended as a temporary arrangement. The strategic decision had already been made that the much-changed, much-expanded and much-modernized ex-Glas factory at Dingolfing was to become the home of the 5-Series. Although it was not yet ready for occupation in mid-1972 when the first of the 5-Series automobiles were assembled, full flow assembly started there in 1973. Before the end of the century, Dingolfing would be producing several other BMW ranges too, and would, in fact, be producing more automobiles every year than any other BMW plant.

Although the energy crisis of 1973, the oil supply embargoes which followed, and the loss of confidence that resulted from all this hit hard at the world's automotive industry, BMW seemed to suffer less than most. Not only did new models continue to pour out of the plants, but sales were little affected. In 1973 BMW

With so little spare space at Munich, the only way to add new office space was to build upwards. Hence what was always affectionately known as the "Four cylinder" building took shape, and was finally opened in 1973.

ABOVE

Body shell manufacture at Milbertshofen always looked complex, and a great deal of jigging and welding was needed. This was 1970.

ABOVE RIGHT

A great occasion at Milberstshofen—the building of the Millionth "New Class" sedan, a 2000. Other celebrations, like this, would certainly follow.

built 197,446 automobiles, in 1974 this sagged to 188,965, but in 1975 it soared again to 221,298. The only high-profile casualty was the 2002 Turbo, BMW's first turbocharged road automobile, which was launched at exactly the wrong moment—September 1973—and was dropped within a year. In the next few years, BMW's product line expanded steadily, and more and more engine and transmission options were added to the line up, which means that it becomes progressively more and more difficult to describe where the automobiles are made, and how they came to be located there.

In the years covered in this chapter—which effectively covers the early 1970s to the 1980s—BMW not only established the three product lines for which they were most noted—the 3-

Series, 5-Series and 7-Series—but they also brought production of their sports coupes back in-house, dabbled with the building of mid-engined "Supercars," and even became a much respected supplier of turbocharged F1 engines. According to textbook economics it was desirable that each of these ranges should be made only in one location but, as we shall see, this was not always possible.

Almost from the start of this period Munich, it seems, was beginning to burst at the seams and BMW was constantly looking forward to build more automobiles, or in different places. Corporate policy, however, was that Munich should concentrate on building the smaller automobiles, with other, larger, models being relocated as and when necessary. As we have already seen, in the early 1970s the ageing "02" automobiles (1602, 1802, 2002, derivatives, sedans, cabriolets and Tourings) all took shape in Munich—the cabriolet body shells being supplied by the independent concern Baur, of Stuttgart. Munich was also the home of the big 2500/2800/Bavaria models, but fortunately true mass-production of the new 5-Series was concentrated on Dingolfing. Even so more, much more, was to be added to the pot in the near future. Not only was the old "02" series soon to be replaced by the very first of the 3-Series models, but what had been a simple little CKD assembly plant in South Africa was about to become more significant in the BMW empire. BMW South Africa was founded in 1973—when Karmann (which was still building sports coupes) was gradually falling out of favor.

Let's start with the arrival of the original 3-Series, the

By the late 1960s, the Milbertshofen factory complex was bursting at the seams, with original "New Class" types, and the first of the "02" models all jostling for space. Here, examples of both types dive into the dip bath in the paint shop.

automobile that would soon become BMW's best-selling automobile—for the original, and future generations, sold in their millions. Right from the start, Munich was always designated as the main 3-Series production plant—and it still is, even to this day, although 3-Series assembly is also to be found at Leipzig, Regensburg, and Rosslyn in South Africa. It was typical of BMW's "can-do" nature that the first 3-Series sedans were built in the summer of 1975—the very first rolled out on June 12, 1975—but the very last of the "02" models was not produced until the end of 1976 (these carried on going into North America for some time). For the time being, by the way, the 3-Series had a choice of gasoline engine sizes, and of carburetor or fuel injection tune engines—though for the moment each and every automobile was a two-door sedan. More than 43,000 such automobiles were built before the end of 1975. This, though, was only the beginning...

We must not forget that the 6-cylinder-engined automobiles were also building up their market share against the might of Mercedes-Benz, nor that from 1971 there were new derivatives of the engines. First of all there would be a 3.0-liter instead of a 2.8-liter, then Bosch fuel injection would be added for some models, and finally there would be a 3.3-liter version, too. All this was achieved from a single engine manufacturing complex at Milbertshofen.

Less than an hour's autobahn drive away from Munich, towards the northeast, the brand-new Dingolfing plant soon got into its stride, and began to produce a gratifying, and highly profitable, number of different 5-Series types. Although these automobiles had originally only been built with 4-cylinder 2.0-liter engines, from 1977 BMW astonished the European motoring world by announcing another brand new line of "small" 6-cylinder engines—which were also to be manufactured at Milbertshofen. Originally fitted to 5-Series automobiles, they were later applied to the 3-Series as well, for the engine bay in those automobiles had always been fashioned to accept the new power unit. This engine, more than any other, tells its own story,

This was the point in the assembly process which every factory visitor to Milbersthofen wanted to see— when the painted body shell was mated to its engine, transmission and suspension. This was an 1800, and the year was 1967.

FAR LEFT
Seat manufacture always took place in a separate department, close to the main assembly lines.

LEFT
BMW 5-Series body shells stacked up as they went through the assembly process at Dingolfing in 1977.

and in particular the long-term way in which BMW planned its future. It must be stressed that it was totally different from the earlier "six," which remained in production; the new version was smaller, lighter, and clearly designed with an eye to a very long life.

And what a life: although almost every detail was changed as time passed, the 6-cylinder gasoline engines produced at Milbertshofen in the 2000s were still recognizably descended from the originals of 1977. Along the way, of course, a single overhead camshaft had given way to a twin-cam layout, two-valves per cylinder gave way to four-valves, turbocharged versions appeared and—a long-way down the "evolution" line —a radically different diesel type would also be developed.

Originally produced as a 122bhp 2.0-liter unit, the new 6-cylinder engine soon began to "stretch" and become more powerful. By the time of the final expansion in the early 2000s, it had reached 3.2-liters, and in M3 form could produce up to 350bhp. Even on my most recent visit to Milbertshofen, in 2008, this engine was still being made in large numbers—and was powering some of the most desirable automobiles in the BMW range.

By the late 1970s Milbertshofen, incidentally, was about to gain a breathing space, for after a nine-year existence the large 6-cylinder-engined automobiles were about to be pensioned off. No fewer than 217,645 such automobiles had been produced, but they were about to be replaced by the first-generation of 7-

Only a decade after BMW had taken control of Glas's small and simple plant at Dingolfing, the factory had been vastly expanded, and a mass of high-tech equipment, including welding robots, installed.

OPPOSITE TOP
Not a human being in sight, as body shells inch there way through the paint shop process in 1977.

OPPOSITE BELOW
The production line in 1973 with BMW 2002 Turbos waiting the have their front spoilers fitted. Even to the modern eye these cars look great.

Series models. Dingolfing, on the other hand, was looking for business. With all traces of the old Glas now swept away, and with a modern BMW factory promising yet more jobs than ever, it still had spare capacity and was a plant for which the company had great ambitions. Accordingly, it came as no surprise that when the new 7-Series automobiles were introduced their new home was to be here, alongside the 5-Series.

Technically the 7-Series was a direct evolution of the original 2500/2800/3.0/3.3-liter types (the last of those automobiles was produced at Milbertshofen in February 1977, after which the facilities were immediately cleared, and re-jigged, to allow yet

more 3-Series automobiles be built there), but in a completely new, all-steel four-door monocoque shell. Engines, transmissions, and all-independent suspension looked familiar to BMW watchers, as did the faithful retention of the double-kidney front-end grille style.

Yet here, as with the 5-Series, was a further statement of the way that BMW intended to do business in the future. Having chosen Dingolfing as the home of the 5-Series, BMW also intended it to be the home of the 7-Series at the same time. Rolls of sheet steel would come into the plant by freight train—there was a main line passing close to the plant—panels would be

THE LAMBORGHINI CONNECTION—SHORT AND TURBULENT

When BMW came to develop the new M1 "supercar" in the late 1970s, it was faced with a familiar dilemma. Who could engineer the automobile quickly, and where could they find space to build just 400 automobiles in a short time? For a company used to evolving automobiles in millions, this was an almost insoluble conundrum that they had never before had to face. Accordingly, BMW cast around to find a respected consultant company that could take on the job for them, and one that would give the project its undivided attention. As a result, BMW's board gave its approval for the building of an exciting mid-engined two-seater in 1976, with the aim of producing a world-beating racing sports car. Originally the new automobile, coded M1 (Motorsport GmBH, Project No. 1), was to be engineered by Lamborghini of Sant' Agata, Italy, with design/style by Ital Design's Giorgetto Giugiaro. Then, when the prototypes had proved themselves, Lamborghini would build all the automobiles on BMW's behalf.

Lamborghini, in fact, was an obvious choice for such a co-operative job, as they were still financially independent of other automobile makers or industrial groups. The comapny had originally been set up by tractor manufacturing millionaire Ferruccio Lamborghini in the early 1960s—the legend is that he had owned Ferrari road automobiles, regularly suffered poor reliability and service from the factory, and was at daggers-drawn with founder Enzo Ferrari himself. The very first Lamborghini road automobile—the 350GT—went on sale in 1963, the sensational mid-engined Miura followed in 1966, and the equally stunning mid-engined Countach made its debut in 1971.

Because Ferruccio Lamborghini himself was rich, and wanted to see a good job done really well, not only did he commission top-class engineers to produce his automobiles, but he also built a brand-new factory at Sant' Agata, which was only a few miles away from Modena and Maranello (where Maserati and Ferrari automobiles were already being built). It was a complex that was soon building front-engined machinery like the Espada, along with exotic mid-engined sports coupes like the Countach and the Urraco. Although the chassis came in from suppliers in the region (there were plenty of those close to Bologna), Lamborghini manufactured its own engines; bodies came from legendary suppliers such as Bertone. Not only were Lamborghini's premises modern, but under-used (their own-brand automobiles were not selling as well as hoped), and the engineering

team could theoretically concentrate on BMW's own needs for a time—and they had no fractious parent company to distract them.

To be sure, this was a good plan, but within a year it all fell to pieces. Although Lamborghini got on rapidly with the job by engineering the chassis and liaising with Giugiaro (whose Ital Design studios were based in the Turin area), and had prototypes up and running by the end of 1977, the Italian concern's finances were in a parlous state. Even though they had secured Italian government money to back the project they missed several BMW-imposed deadlines, so in April 1978 BMW was forced to terminate their agreement. Although this meant an almost immediate end to co-operation with Lamborghini, BMW's final solution was complex and ruthlessly efficient. With the M1 project now taken away from the moribund Lamborghini concern, should BMW cancel it completely (and lose face, for all this dirty laundry was being washed in public?), have it built at Munich, or should they get involved in a far more complicated process?

In the end it was Giorgetto Giugiaro himself who influenced the way that the automobiles were built, though not in a way that made BMW's accountants totally happy. First of all, Marchesi of Modena would build the tubular chassis frames and suspension units, these would then be sent to Ital Design of Turin where ten-section molded GRP body shells from Transformazione Italiana Resina were built up, bonded and riveted, before the assembly was then painted and glazed. Structures would then be transported (by truck) to Baur of Stuttgart (Baur, of course, was one of BMW's most favored suppliers), who undertook complete and final assembly, using engines from BMW of Munich, transmissions from ZF, and many other components from the BMW parts bin. When M1s were finally made ready to be road-tested, they were then sent on to BMW Motorsport for final "snagging" and pre-delivery work. Because of the complicated nature of the build process, it was not surprising that much tweaking often had to be done before the automobiles were finally sold !

Although the M1 went on to have a gratifying high-profile career (a one-model Championship at Grand Prix weekends in 1979 and 1980 reaped an enormous amount of publicity), the way in which it was built was never repeated by BMW. All new-automobile projects, henceforth, would be tackled in-house.

CLOCKWISE FROM TOP LEFT
Fitting out an early example of the 3-Series cars, as introduced at Milbertshofen in the mid-1970s.

Cars cannot entirely be built by machinery—human beings, flexible and resourceful, will always be needed. This was 3-Series manufacture in the Munich factory in 1975.

Body shell assembly in the mid-1970s. No wonder style changes were made at infrequent intervals.

The ex-Glas factory at Dingolfing was hugely expanded and modernised in the early 1970s, soon coming to concentrate on 5-Series assembly. This was the very first six-cylinder engined 525, on the body assembly lines in January 1973.

pressed on site, and monocoques would be assembled, painted and trimmed. The rest of the running gear would be supplied from other BMW plants, not least the big 6-cylinder engines coming up the road, just an hour's autobahn journey away, from Milbertshofen. Then, as in later years, completed automobiles would be delivered by rail to distribution centers, or to ports for trans-shipment to important markets like North America. It all made a great deal of sense: small automobiles to be built in Munich; bigger automobiles in Dingolfing; components to be supplied from all round the country. But there was still one oddity that needed to be sorted out: the production of sports coupes at Karmann, whose factory at Osnabruck was 415 miles/670 kilometers from Bavaria, in the opposite corner of West Germany.

Karmann, of course, had built the first-generation 4-cylinder 2000CS coupes from 1965, and had smoothly converted its assembly lines to produce the 6-cylinder derivatives when they were introduced in 1968. These new automobiles were effectively conversions of the 2000CS, but with a longer nose/longer wheelbase—this being the quick, effective and very accomplished way in which Karmann could do business at the time. In all cases, BMW delivered running gear from Munich to Osnabruck (or the suppliers delivered direct from their own premises), before Karmann completed the assembly and returned the results, as finished products, for BMW to feed into their dealer chain. From 1971 these automobiles were once again re-engineered under the skin, now having complete 6-cylinder automobile running gear and rear ends, including four-wheel disc brakes and much more powerful engines—including fuel-injected types. When BMW decided to go further into sports car racing, and needed light-alloy panels, with aerodynamic kits to add down-force at speed, Karmann was once again the ideal concern to tackle the job.

BMW, however, was not convinced that the build quality of Karmann's products was always up to their demanding standards, and cast around for an alternative. But was there an alternative? In Germany, probably the only sensible alternative source for specialist automobiles like this would be at Baur, in Stuttgart, but Baur had other commitments to other clients, and could not cope. The answer, in fact, was found close to home—in fact at Dingolfing. When the well-liked coupes of 1965–75 were finally dropped, they were replaced by the first of a new BMW line—the 6-Series automobiles. These smart 2+2 seaters were based on an entirely new pressed steel platform that, though it was not spelt out at the time, was itself based on the platform of the still-secret 7-Series, which would follow in 1977.

Robots getting to work at the factory in the late 1970s

Accordingly, while all the new press tooling, weld and assembly machinery connected with the new automobiles were installed together at Dingolfing, it was the 6-Series that was ready for launch a year before the sedans arrived. This happens often in the world's motor industry: a "specialty" model goes into production before the more mass-market automobile on which it is based, so that manufacturing engineers can work through a settling-down period at a measured pace. For the time being (and as it had always done with the original Coupes), BMW supplied platforms and sub-assemblies for the new 6-Series to Karmann in Osnabruck. Karmann completed the body shells, painted and trimmed them, then assembled the entire automobiles complete with running gear supplied from Bavaria, before sending them back 415 miles/670 kilometers to Dingolfing, by train, for final checks and delivery. Since 1965, when the first 2000CS had appeared, this had never been an ideal arrangement. It had only been justified by a lack of capacity in BMW's own plants, but by the late 1970s it made very little sense at all. Accordingly, no soon had the 7-Series been launched in 1977, than BMW took final assembly of 6-Series automobiles back in-house at Dingolfing (although body shells

By 1979, BMW assembly was still expanding steadily, with at least 1,000 cars being completed every day.

In the early 1980s, one of the last detail jobs in building a BMW was to add, and screw into place, the headlamps.

continued to be manufactured by Karmann).

Ten years after BMW had originally taken over the corporate wreckage of the Glas company (in 1967), the transformation at Dingolfing was complete. Except as a trademark name in the archives (and, for sure, as a fond memory in the minds of many Dingolfing residents), Glas no longer existed. BMW's new factory had been in use since 1973 and now, only four years later, it was already manufacturing three different model lines—the 5-Series, 6-Series and 7-Series. Remarkable.

Steyr—the diesel revolution

Nowadays, as is well known, BMW make some of the most powerful, torquey and environmentally "green" diesel engines in the world, yet the company did not put its very first diesel automobile on sale until the 1980s. Before the 1970s it was really only Mercedes-Benz and BMW who had taken the diesel engine seriously, and it was not for nothing that those automobiles

became whimsically known as "Stuttgart taxis." Then came the Energy Crisis, and the huge hike in oil prices that followed in 1974 and 1975. It was in the aftermath of these cataclysmic events that Europe's automobile makers began to take diesel-engined automobiles seriously. BMW, though, took time to investigate their options. As is now well known, the first-ever diesel-engined BMW private automobile was the 324d of 1985, but development work had been in hand for some years before that.

In the meantime BMW had bowed to the inevitable—if they were to keep pushing ahead with automobile assembly at Munich/Milbertshofen, then they were running out of space and would have to move more and more operations elsewhere. Currently every engine that powered every BMW automobile was manufactured in the historic old factory in Munich, and no more could be done to ease the congestion. By this time, more than 1,200 engines were being produced in Munich every day—this was almost three times as many as had conservatively been forecast just a decade earlier—in no fewer than 200 different types and sub-derivatives. With demand for all three of the major automobile product lines—3-Series, 5-Series and 7-Series—continuing to increase, it would soon be essential to open up a new engine plant.

After an extensive search, the choice fell on Steyr in Upper Austria, which was around 200 miles/322 kilometers east of Munich and close to the city of Linz. The ancient city of Steyr lies at the confluence of the Steyr and Enns rivers and is connected to Munich, via Salzburg, by autobahn. It had a long history of manufacturing, and is the home of the Steyr-Mannlicher arms company and Steyr tractors and automobiles. BMW began work on building a dedicated engine plant at Steyr in 1979, and the first gasoline engines were produced there in 1982—but it was as a diesel engine production plant that Steyr became most famous. Expansion followed expansion, and every mainstream BMW diesel engine has been manufactured there such that by the end of the 1990s Steyr had become the largest producer of BMW engines in the world.

BELOW LEFT
In modern times, windscreens are applied automatically to a new car's body shell, but in 1981 it was still a skilled job for a technician to undertake.

BELOW RIGHT
Almost through the paint shop process, in 1981 this body shell gets a final polish before it is sent to the final assembly lines to meet all its mechanical equipment.

RIGHT

"Doors-off" build technology is now recognised throughout the world's car-making factories, but BMW was one of the first to apply it to their cars. The car is a 3-Series, the date is 1982, and the location is the Milbertshofen plant.

RIGHT

Once the New Class sedans were well established, BMW could then indulge themselves in developing sporty versions—such as the 2000 CS Coupe. Launched in 1965, the originals had 2-liter four-cylinder engines, but larger, six-cylinder, versions would follow later.

RIGHT

Once rebuilt and re-equipped, the ex-Glas plant at Dingolfing became one of BMW's most productive plants. Here the two millionth BMW to be produced at that plant was completed on 2 March 1987.

CENTER

In the 1980s, this was how and where a painted and partly-trimmed 3-Series body shell was mated with its running gear.

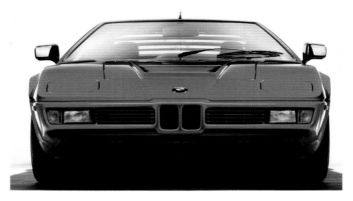

LEFT
The mid-engined M1 was originally conceived as a racing sports car, but BMW put it into limited production at the end of the 1970s.

BELOW
The entire front end assembly of a 5-Series (Type E34), engine, cross-member and MacPherson strut front suspension, being readied for assembly at Dingolfing.

Once the Steyr engine plant had been established in Austria, demand for engines, and therefore of more factory space, was unstoppable. Phase III expansion, therefore, was well under way in 1987.

Body shell assembly in profusion, at Munich in 1989.

Steyr was not only at the hub of engine assembly, it also became a supplier of machined components to other engine plant (including, from 2001, the British Ham's Hall factory), and in turn it relied on the supply of specialized components from Landshut (and a major foundry), Munich and Berlin. How to measure the size and worth of this Austrian mammoth? By two statistics: it produced more than 3,000 engines every day, from a workforce of more than 2,600 people.

All set for the 1980s

As the 1980s dawned, BMW was firmly set on the road to expansion. Annual output of private automobiles had risen above the 300,000 mark (and was still going up, steadily), two centers of final assembly—Munich/Milbertshofen and Dingolfing—were now firmly established, while major supplies flowed in from plants as diverse as Spandau (Berlin), Landshut (Bavaria), Karmann (northern Germany) and Steyr (Austria). This, though, was only one stage in the inexorable growth that was to follow. Not only was BMW looking to build half-a-million automobiles a year by the 1990s (and more, and more...), but it had ambitions to start building in North America too. Would it be a bumpy ride?

LEFT
Many years ago the town of Steyr was solely known for the make of Austrian car produced there, but by the 1980s BMW had developed a massive new engine plant adding to the town's fame.

BMW celebrated the building of the 10,000th engine at Steyr in January 1983—this being a six-cylinder M20-type unit.

ABOVE
Steyr built its 500,000th engine in 1987. Here it is being slotted into place in a 3-Series model.

RIGHT
The plaque on the engine commemorating that fact.

By the late 1980s, BMW's foundry process at the Milbertshofen, in Munich, was a highly-mechanised process.

UNSTOPPABLE

CHAPTER 10

OPENING UP IN NORTH AMERICA

L OOKING BACK, IT WAS REALLY ONLY A MATTER OF TIME BEFORE BMW decided to build an assembly plant in North America. After a slow start in the 1950s, their sales in that continent had been rising steadily for some time and with BMW now in such a confident mood in the 1990s—the brand was now about to expand into two-seater sports cars (the Z3) and four-wheel-drive SAVs (the X5)—factory space was again at a premium.

Once again, BMW's automobile output figures in this period speak for themselves. In 1990, the German factories had produced 503,000 automobiles, with 16,500 automobiles coming from the Rosslyn plant in South Africa. Four years later, the German figures had increased to 557,000 and, although the output from Rosslyn output was still low at 16,500, BMW was moving rapidly towards "house full." The fact that the company had just taken over the Rover/Land Rover group brought its own particular problems. Although the three principal German factories—Milbertshofen (Munich), Dingolfing, and Regensburg—were already approaching their current capacity constraints, and although the Rover/Land Rover purchase looked promising at the time, there was neither spare capacity nor the intention to produce BMWs in Britain.

At Spartanburg, in the USA, BMW assembly is so flexible that two-seater Roadsters can take shape in between X5 SAVs.

Despite production restraints, BMW seemed to be determined to break out of the long-term stability of its product range—sedans, estates, coupes and convertibles in a variety of sizes, but little more. Behind closed doors, in Munich, ambitious bosses were looking at the sports car, and the SUV markets—both of which seemed to be booming, and in neither of which was BMW currently represented. The ambition was certainly there. If Mercedes-Benz could make good money, and boost their reputation, with automobiles like the SL series, then BMW could surely do the same? Not only that, but if a number of the world's biggest automobile makers—notably Ford, Jeep, Nissan and Toyota—could all produce fast, roomy, civilized and (above all) capable four-wheel-drive wagons (SUVs), then BMW lusted after a big share of that business. In both cases, the bulk of the business to be gleaned would come from North America. At the time, need I add, BMW can have had no idea that their biggest and, in some ways their most bitter rival, Daimler-Benz, was coming to the same conclusions at the same time. It can surely be no coincidence that the Mercedes-Benz SLK would be launched soon after the Z3 Roadster, while the Mercedes-Benz ML SUV appeared in 1997.

Design and development was one thing, of course, but space

North America has plenty of space to establish large assembly plants—as this aerial study of the Spartanburg factory makes clear. Assembly of Z3 Roadsters began in 1995.

and capability for manufacturing was quite another. Quite simply, early in the 1990s BMW had nowhere in Europe where such new models could be put into production—and in the case of four-wheel-drive SUVs they lacked the design and development expertise too. Four-wheel-drive BMW private automobiles had, of course, already been put on sale, but these were not intended for off road motoring. This, make no mistake, was one very good reason why BMW was so happy to get its hands on the Rover Group business in Great Britain (I describe this episode in BMW's business development in the next chapter), for Land Rover had been building 4x4s since 1948, had a sound reputation at all price levels, and was looking to expand that business in the future.

American opportunity

Early in the 1990s, the decision to build a new assembly plant outside Germany was a huge gamble. Previously BMW, like Mercedes-Benz, had taken pride in building German automobiles in the German way... in Germany. For BMW, the only previous exception to this had been in South Africa, where (because of the imposition of high import duties) it made sense to assemble automobiles in the country where they would be sold. In the end it was the decision of Japanese concerns—notably Honda, Mazda and Nissan—to set up local assembly in the United States that tipped the balance. Not only had the Japanese concluded that there was good business to be done in that country, but any number of attractive financial packages were being offered as an extra incentive. If the Japanese could do it, thought BMW, then so could they. There was, in any case, another factor. Before the end of the 1980s, German luxury automobile makers like BMW and Mercedes-Benz were suffering in the North American market, not only because the German currency was flying so high, but because a newcomer—the Japanese Lexus—was hitting them so hard. BMW's North American importers advised, with increasing urgency, that American buyers had little product loyalty, would vote with their cash books only, and would come back to BMW only if the price was right.

BMW therefore made a vital double decision—not only would they establish a brand-new manufacturing site (it would have been possible to "buy in" to an existing, but redundant, automotive plant in North America, but that was not the BMW way...), but they would also begin building a new product line there too. It would have been easy to elect to produce 3-Series and 5-Series models—more of the same, in other words, but for

BMW decided to produce its first mass-market two-seater, specifically to appeal to North Americans.

Once begun, the search for a new North American home was intense. Not only would the geographical location need to be right, but so would the transport/freightage links with Europe. How important was it that the chosen workforce should have experience in making automobiles—especially of the high quality which BMW expected? Clearly it was vital that a potential workforce was immediately available. Each and every state of the Union was visited, and many of them offered an intriguing package of financial incentives. Even so, it was not until 1992 that a site was chosen at Spartanburg, a relatively small city (population around 50,000) in South Carolina, which was just 90 minutes' drive from Charlotte and about 200 miles/322 kilometers inland from the useful commercial port of Charleston, where many of BMW's imported components would be unloaded.

Once a new company—BMW Manufacturing Co.—had been set up, and the deal had been done with the local authorities, construction on the 1,150-acre site (2.5 million square feet/0.25 million square meters were developed) went ahead at breakneck pace. In the end BMW could not only claim that this was their first full manufacturing site outside Germany and—by definition—their first in North America, but that it had all been done to an astonishingly compressed schedule. The ambitious Spartanburg factory project was revealed in June 1992, the initial groundbreaking ceremony took place on September 30, 1992, and the very first completed automobile rolled off the lines on September 8, 1994. Wisely, though not as a long-term intention, BMW decided to start up the operation effectively as a shakedown exercise, by using it initially as an assembly plant for 3-Series kits that had been sent out from Germany, well before the first of the two-seaters (the Z3) was ready for launch. Accordingly, the very first completed automobile was a four-door 318i sedan for delivery to an American customer. As the company later confirmed, with great pride, the initial development of this 1,150-acre site had been achieved in record time and the first automobiles had been delivered in just 23 months, from construction start to first-automobile delivery.

By any standards BMW—notably a cautious company in all its projects, all its forecasts, and all its before-the-event claims—had taken risks in setting up Spartanburg. Here was a site and a part of the US that had absolutely no previous automobile-building (engineering, even) heritage. Nor was Spartanburg even geographically close to any other US site with automotive expertize. In BMW's own experience, it certainly could not be

compared with a recent factory opening at Regensburg—which was, at least, in Bavaria, geographically close to Dingolfing, and less than two hours' drive from downtown Munich. Not that this deterred the potential workforce. When job openings were first advertised no fewer than 85,000 locals applied, though only 1,700 were initially hired. The workforce rapidly grew, such that when the X5 was also in full production more than 4,000 associates were being employed. Wisely, when the plant opened BMW did not immediately impose a plant manager from Germany, but hired Al Kinser, the American specialist who had been the first manager of the North American Honda assembly

Z3 Roadster assembly getting under way at BMW's brand-new assembly plant at Spartanburg, South Carolina, in 1995. Within ten years, Spartanburg was also looking after X5 SAV assembly too.

As ever in a BMW motor manufacturing plant, robots have almost taken over from people—this being the paint shop at the Spartanburg plant.

2007 it was well over $3 billion, though the start-up had been on a more modest scale. Although the plant found its feet by assembling 3-Series sedans, this was purely to get a new workforce used to the sort of automobiles that BMW liked to build, and it soon changed over to the real reason for building a new plant—the manufacture of a new-generation of two-seater roadsters. The BMW Z3 was a conventional sports car specifically designed to appeal to the American market. It had two seats, conservative styling, a lightly-tuned 4-cylinder engine (other engines would follow), and a unit-construction platform based closely on that of the latest BMW 3-Series Compact (the Compact had a shorter wheelbase than the four-door 3-Series sedans of the period). It retained the old-type semi-trailing arm independent rear suspension of that model, and was therefore "old technology" as far as Munich was concerned. BMW, of course, wanted it to be that way, not only because they wanted to bring it in at a sensible price, but because they also wanted it to be an easily-assembled entry-level automobile. It was not meant to be a tire-stripping monster to compete with the most highly specified Chevrolet Corvette—it was an automobile that a young American man or woman could enjoy driving, yet could find it straightforward to insure. In addition, the use of a new Z3 by "James Bond" in the 1995 movie *Goldeneye* was a great coup for BMW—as was the extension of the movie deal to include the use of a 750iL, and a Z8 in later productions. By comparison with other Bond automobiles, such as the Aston Martin that had been seen in earlier films, the Z3 was no great performer. But according to the script it was well equipped with all the usual Bond gimmicks, including Stinger missiles. Apparently there were rich American customers who wanted to know if their Z3 could have those accessories added...

plant in Ohio.

Spartanburg's original vice-president was Karl Flescher, who had earlier been BMW-USA's marketing chief, and he made the point that there had been some difficulty in picking the correct workforce for what had been a new "greenfield" site:

"There were high risks and potentially massive problems, such as marrying together many different cultures. We had people who'd worked at Japanese factories in the U.S., non-car workers, and German staff from BMW. We knew we could not make a car that did not hit German standards."

A first two-seater sports car: the Z3

By the beginning of the new century, BMW's investment in Spartanburg was on its way towards $2 billion dollars, and by

One factor that apparently caused the strategists to take much time in planning the Spartanburg facility was: how many automobiles a year could be sold, and how many of the components that went into those automobiles could be manufactured in North America? If potential sales were low, then little more than an assembly plant for imported pieces would be justified (Spartanburg, in other words, would be little more than a "screw-driver" plant assembling automobiles from German-built CKD packs). However, the more those sales forecasts rose, the easier it would be to justify the laying down of duplicate facilities to those existing in Europe. Because it looked as if the Z3 would sell at between 50,000 and 70,000 units a year, there was no economic case for manufacturing much of the running gear—engines, transmissions and steering gear in particular—in the United States, so these were imported, by the

ABOVE

The X5 SAV was an ideal new BMW model for sale in the US market, so it made logical sense to assemble it at the new Spartanburg factory in South Carolina.

ship-load, to deep water ports on the Eastern Seaboard. Pressed elements of the 3-Series Compact platform would arrive by the same route, though the unique paneling, and body assembly facilities, would take shape at Spartanburg, after which painting and assembly would get under way. Component suppliers of anything from tires to trim panels, and electrical components to service literature, also set up shop in the United States, so there was soon a complex ordering/supply/fitment operation that soon looked just like those of any other BMW plant in Europe.

In the beginning, the plant was laid out for a maximum throughput of 300 automobiles a day—1,500 automobiles a week, or up to 70,000 automobiles a year—but it took time for those figures to be approached. When they were published, some years later, BMW's own figures tell a very significant story. It took two years for the first 100,000 Z3s to be completed, but

ABOVE

Difficult to quite work out what is going on? In fact the body shell of this BMW, at the Spartanburg plant, is being positioned on its side, so that the worker can add components to the underside without having to strain his body.

LEFT

Having been painted at Spartanburg, a Z4 Roadster and an X5 SUV are just starting the final assembly process.

the company then announced that production of the radically new four-wheel-drive X5 Sport Activity Vehicle (SAV) would soon be added to the line up, at which point overall sales were expected to double. Even so, according to BMW's then Chairman, Bernd Pischetsrieder, there was never any intention to assemble Land Rovers and Range Rovers in this new facility. As with other BMW plants, the product mix coming out of the gates at Spartanburg soon became wide-ranging. The 4-cylinder Z3s were soon joined by 6-cylinder Z3s, a truly ferocious M3-engined version soon followed, and shortly after this there was also a permanent hard-top/hatchback derivative, which (if BMW was honest) was not the prettiest automobile its design studios had ever produced. The 250,000th Z3 was built on February 12, 2001.

The four-wheel-drive BMW X5

Then, of course, there was the four-wheel-drive X5, whose natural home was surely Spartanburg, if only because the majority of sales were bound to be made in North America. As I make very clear in the next chapter, although BMW had had four-wheel-drive/SAV ambitions for some time they lacked experience, so the acquisition of Land Rover in 1994 provided a welcome boost—and the X5 appeared five years down the road. For BMW, the choice of Spartanburg to build X5s was very significant, and to BMW-watchers, who realized that such decisions were rarely taken in a hurry, it was clear that the location of this very important project had been decided some time earlier. At the time, and all round the world, BMW was rapidly running out of space in which to build entirely new model ranges—and the SUV sector was becoming increasingly important.

By 1996, when the Z3 was finally in full volume production, BMW could concentrate on getting the X5 ready to join it at Spartanburg. In 1995, no fewer than 583,000 BMWs had been produced in Germany and South Africa, and although the sales force was sure that it could move more metal, all but the Spartanburg plants were bursting at the seams. It was, therefore, a great relief to plan to introduce the new X5, to locate its production in the USA—and to expect to sell a high proportion of the output in that nation.

Until the X5 was designed, BMW had never before built an automobile of this type (I ignore the limited-production military-only 325 "scout car" of 1937). Although four-wheel-drive 3-Series and 5-Series derivatives had been on sale for some time, these were not meant to provide ultimate go-anywhere off-road

Although much of the body shell of the Z3 Coupe was unique, it was assembled on the same tracks as the Z3 Roadster at Spartanburg.

Showing off the flexibility of the plant, painted shells for a Z4 Roadster, and an X5 SAV, sit side by side, waiting for final assembly to begin.

OPPOSITE
This partly complete Z4 Roadster body shell on the production line at Spartanburg, USA.

123

performance, which was what the X5 aimed to do. Although much of the X5's basic suspension and choice of engines was shared with the existing 7-Series sedan, the new off-roader got an entirely new floor-pan and, of course, four-wheel-drive installation. It was significant that in August 1999, when the new vehicle was launched, BMW insisted that original development had begun before the Rover/Land Rover purchase—which of course included Range Rover—was made in 1994. Except for the use of corporate engines (which counted as ultimate "building blocks" in the modern motor industry) BMW also insisted that nothing of significance to be found in the next generation Range Rover (which was due for launch in a year's time) was shared with the X5.

Series production of X5s began at Spartanburg in September 1999, just days after technical details were released. At this time, BMW stated that between 40,000 and 45,000 X5s would be built in a year, and that although these machines would share the same paint shop, the same U.S. supplier-chain, and the same delivery of engines and transmissions, by ship, from Europe, they would be assembled on completely different lines. To their obvious pleasure, BMW found the X5 selling just as well as hoped, and celebrated the building of 100,000th example in August 2001, which was almost exactly two years after the first automobile had dropped off the line at Spartanburg. From then, it was certain, the future of Spartanburg was assured, though the products it was to build would be kept entirely separate from the company's European products.

Accordingly, when the time came to replace the original Z3 sports roadster with a Z4, there was never any question about the location of its manufacture—it would, of course, be produced at Spartanburg. Assembly of Z3s ended on June 28, 2002, after which there was then a sizeable gap while re-jigged facilities were installed for the first new-generation Z4s to be assembled in South Carolina. In the meantime, and just to emphasize the way that their Stateside enterprise was booming, BMW also celebrated the building of the 500,000th Spartanburg automobile in July 2002.

By any standards, the replacement of the Z3 by the Z4 was a major enterprise for BMW—and Spartanburg—for this had not been a simple re-style, or face-lift, on the existing platform. Instead, the Z4 was to be based on a new-generation 3-Series platform, complete with Z-axle rear suspension. Now that it had a real sports car, in the Z4, to write about, the specialist media let rip at the old Z3, stating that it really hadn't been very good, particularly not in dynamic terms—yet they had to admit that with nearly 300,000 automobiles sold in seven years, who on

earth could complain? So what if it hadn't handled like a Porsche Boxster, it was an automobile that had sold particularly well in the United States (where it was built) and brought much profit into BMW's coffers. This time around, and Spartanburg was proud to be building it, the new automobile had up-to-the-minute handling and performance, a much stiffer open-top shell (BMW claimed that it was more than twice as stiff as the Z3 had ever been), and such sales-encouraging details as a six-speed ZF manual transmission, electric power-assisted steering and a startling new style. As we had all come to expect of this type of product, in this country, from this plant, production accelerated smoothly away, sales held up well, the 100,000th Z4 was completed in November 2004, and the success story continued.

After that, BMW was always upbeat about its North American plant, its performance, and the automobiles that it produced in such gratifying numbers. Right from the start, it had been the first US-based auto plant to use water-based (as opposed to high solvent-based) paint in its production process, it gained all manner of environmental awards, and—very important to the staff's self-esteem—it was the exclusive manufacturer of Z3/Z4 roadsters, and X5 SAV ranges. There was no back up of alternative assembly lines or, at the time, any threat to move them out of the US. Thus when in September 2006 the second-generation X5 was launched—new style, new engines, new six-speed automatic transmission, better on-road handling characteristics than the original—the latest type was to be produced solely at Spartanburg. A year after that BMW's new X6, an automobile with the latest X5's platform and choice of running gears, also went into production at Spartanburg. The X6 had a new cabin that some called a "coupe SAV" and which all were happy to describe as a "crossover" type of model, which was then fashionable.

Corporate planning, however, never seemed to stand still at BMW, because within months of that release—and when X5/X6 sales appeared to be so buoyant—BMW revealed that the successor to the existing Z4 would not be built at Spartanburg, but in Europe, though a date for the new model was not announced. Despite that, in 2008 the company announced a further investment of $750 million in the Spartanburg plant, which would increase its size by 60 percent, and would raise capacity to 240,000 vehicles a year by 2012. X3s, it was suggested, would be assembled in the new buildings. After a cautious beginning, therefore, Spartanburg was reaching maturity, and was clearly to be an established part of BMW's Group Production network, which now covered so much of the globe.

SPORTS CARS—THE Z CARS

Then, as now, North American buyers have always loved two-seater sports cars, whether domestically built or imported from Europe and Japan. In the beginning there were British Triumphs, MGs and Austin-Healeys, then there were Japanese Nissans and Hondas—and from the 1980s there were BMWs. Although BMW had already produced a few—a very few—328s and 507s, until the 1980s the company had never produced what I might call a mass-market two-seater. It was only then that the Z-car pedigree was invented. Since that time, Z1, Z3, Z4 and Z8 types have all been put on the market, and others have been trialed. All have had conventional front-engine/rear-drive layouts.

The first of the line was the Z1 of 1988, a 2.5-liter/6-cylinder engined machine, which featured doors which did not open outwards or upwards in conventional ways, but that could be retracted downwards into capacious body sills. This was the first BMW road automobile, incidentally, to have what was colloquially called the "Z-axle" variety of independent rear suspension. Between 1988 and 1991, only 8,000 were produced in Germany.

Z3 was a conventional two-seater put into production at the brand-new North American factory at Spartanburg, South Carolina, in 1995, based on the platform of the 3-Series Compact hatchback, and available with many different 4-cylinder and 6-cylinder engines. Top of the range was a highly tuned Z3M type, and there was also a fixed-head coupe/hatchback derivative. After almost 300,000 had been produced, the Z3 was eventually supplanted at Spartanburg by the Z4 in 2002.

Z4 featured a more flamboyant style, and was based on the platform of the contemporary 3-Series sedan (which meant that it had Z-axle rear suspension). It took over at Spartanburg in 2002, and in the next few years was built with a whole variety of 4-cylinder and 6-cylinder engines. The Z8 of 2000 was directly descended from the ZO7 concept automobile exhibited at the Tokyo Show of 1997 and had been styled at BMW's Designworks in Southern California. Powered by a massive 4.9-liter V8, it featured an aluminum chassis/monocoque, harked back to the old 507 in some visual ways, but was expensive and, somehow, rather uncouth. Only 5,703 automobiles were built at Dingolfing in Munich up until 2003, before the experts at that factory turned their attention to the aluminum-shelled Rolls-Royce Phantom instead.

CHAPTER 11

FALSE START—ROVER, THE ENGLISH PATIENT

B MW's short ownership of the Rover Group is now something that the company has long since shrugged off—especially as it was one of the very few company strategic exercises that failed. The miracle was that BMW was financially strong enough, with a positive overall image, to put it behind them after only six years of relentless struggle.

In the 1990s, the second-generation Range Rover, assembled at Solihull, featured a separate chassis frame, to which the estate-car type of body shell has just been mated.

In the beginning, however, BMW saw this as a commercial opportunity not to be missed—one that would allow them to expand their coverage of the automotive market, and that would provide much-needed factory space. Not only would it present them with a mountain of front-wheel-drive expertise in the shape of the Mini and various Honda-influenced Rover family automobiles, but it would also give them the real prize, of owning the Range Rover/Land Rover brand, and getting access to all its 4x4 expertise. In the early 1990s, BMW was already thinking of developing its first four-wheel-drive SUV model, which would become the X5 of 1999, and the company could immediately see ways of cutting down on time, development expense, and mistakes.

Taking on Rover

By this stage, of course, Rover, its constituents, and its managers, were thoroughly used to the idea of being owned by a different concern, and admired all of them—for a time. The Rover Group, in effect, was like a much-married woman who was ageing, had somehow managed to preserve her looks, and was still attractive to a succession of new suitors over the years. Thus it was that Rover, the battered remnant of the troubled British Leyland colossus, came to BMW's attention in 1993. State-owned from 1975, it had been sold off cheaply to British Aerospace in 1988, who had spent years knocking down old factories and slimming down the business, and was now ready to bail out.

The attraction was not only Rover itself. This rambling group also embraced four other active brands—Land Rover, Range Rover, MG and Mini—while other once-famous names (including Triumph and Austin-Healey) were already in the trademarks locker. There was, at the time, an on-going and valuable technical and financial link with Honda of Japan, which had a 20 percent financial stake in the business. All existing Rover family automobiles (except the Mini and Rover 100) had been derived from Honda types of the period. With several large and under-used factories to support—Longbridge (Birmingham), Solihull (near Birmingham) and Cowley (near Oxford) assembled the automobiles, and were supported by vast pressings plants at Cowley and at Swindon (also near Oxford)— Rover was a loss-making conglomerate, and could not hope to survive on its own. BMW, even so, thought it saw great potential, and was happy to buy it all from British Aerospace for £800 million (approx. $1.4 Billion at the existing rate of exchange). From March 1994, Rover therefore became a wholly owned subsidiary of BMW, the Honda connection was ruthlessly broken off, and BMW moved swiftly to impose its own ideas.

For the next six years BMW invested hugely in Rover, and as an example of good faith, a vast new corporate engine plant was designed and built at Ham's Hall, just a few miles away from Solihull. New-generation BMW gasoline and diesel engines were ear-marked for existing and future Rover Group models, BMW tapped into Land Rover's 4x4 expertise for its own purposes (X5 and X3 both benefited), Rover 75s appeared on BMW company fleets in Germany, and small Rovers came to be used as courtesy automobiles in British BMW dealerships. Unhappily Rover soon became known as the "English patient" (especially in Munich), for profits were never made. BMW invested heavily in a new series of cars including the Rover 75 sedan, the MGF sports car, the Land Rover Freelander, and a new Discovery. Plans were also made for a new mid-sized Rover to replace the 600-Series and a startlingly advanced new generation of Range Rovers. Despite

n the 1990s, Land Rover still built its own engines at the Solihull plant, before BMW began to re-engine the cars to use BMW power plants instead.

Rover's "East Works", at Solihull, was erected in the 1970s, to produce Rover cars. Later it took on Triumph TR7 assembly too. When BMW owned the Rover Group in the 1990s, it was converted into a massive state-of-the-art body plant to build Land Rovers and Range Rovers.

though the Rover design/engineering/development HQ was relocated to the company's test/development centre at Gaydon (southeast of Birmingham), and a mountain of new facilities were commissioned, sales continued to lag.

There were many problems still to be overcome, the most crucial being that the structures of existing assembly plants were all ancient. Longbridge, Rover's HQ, dated back to the early 20th Century with later additions, none of which were less than forty years old, Cowley (Oxford, as BMW insisted in calling it) was really the old Pressed Steel Co. Ltd's body manufacturing plant of the 1920s and 1930s, which had received several expensive makeovers, while the Land Rover plant at Solihull had started life as an aero-engine "shadow factory" during the 1940s, and had been expanded, piecemeal, ever since.

Even so, in addition to all the new projects already

ABOVE
Rover 200s had been assembled at Longbridge since the 1980s, but if BMW had carried on its tenure they would have completely re-jigged the facilities.

LEFT
Rover never stinted on new robot capital equipment in the Longbridge works—this multi-jig being for Rover 200 assembly.

Rover's own 16-valve twin overhead camshaft 1.4/1.6/1.8-litre engine was used in many Rover and Land Rover products during BMW's tenure, but proposals to instal it in the new-generation MINI were not carried forward.

Although Rover's vee-6 layout KV6 power unit was a fine design, BMW considered it too costly to fit in any of their 3-Series range of the day.

mentioned, BMW soon set out to develop a completely new-generation MINI, which was going to involve the largest investment of them all. Although Rover carried out this work very competently, and very speedily, the rest of the Rover Group was still in trouble, so BMW's patience finally snapped. From 1999 more and more German managers were drafted in to impose change, although this was only a short-term strategy for in March 2000 BMW capitulated, and decided to get rid of most of its British investments. Rover, BMW announced, was to be put up for sale, and the best offers would be accepted. After an industrially turbulent period when one potential buyer (the venture capitalist organization of Alchemy Partners) came and went, and when Ford-of-Europe offered to buy the entire Land Rover business but not the complete Rover Group, a deal was finally done in May 2000. BMW, it was said, would sell Land Rover to Ford, would keep the MINI brand for itself (along with the still-secret new model, which was almost ready for launch), and would retain many of the trademark rights to dormant brands. They would then sell the remainder of the Rover Group to a management buy-out team for the princely sum of £10 (a mere $17), absorb all existing debts, and provide the new company with a huge loan as a dowry to make sure that the business was off their hands.

Accordingly, under new ownership Rover (soon to be re-named MG-Rover) would retain the Rover and MG brands, Rover 75 assembly (and all its jigging, tooling and manufacturing equipment) would be up-rooted from Cowley and transferred 60 miles/97 kilometers up the road to Longbridge. BMW, on the other hand, guaranteed to complete work on the MINI project, to dig up all the production equipment just being installed at Longbridge, move it down the road to Cowley, and begin large-scale production there at a plant that they soon renamed BMW-Oxford. A £427 million (around $726 million) "soft" loan, which did not have to be paid back for many years, would be provided to Rover, so that the still loss-making business could stay afloat until it became profitable. Within months, BMW had expunged the Rover experience from its image as though it had never been there, though it cannot have been long before the directors realized that their loans might not have been very wisely made.

The fact is that the Phoenix consortium, led by ex-Rover employee John Towers, always lacked the working capital to carry on investing in Rover in a way that was really essential. Five years later—by which time BMW had not only shrugged off the financial trauma of its British experiment, but also had worldwide sales and production that were reaching new heights—the MG-Rover business that they had sold off was still losing money. It had never made a profit, even at day-to-day operating level, in all that time. The new management had not been able to afford to introduce any important new models (all they could do was tickle up existing automobiles, squander money on motor racing programs, and to indulge themselves in a fantastically ill-advised MG-badged supercar project), struggled to find any partners, and eventually ran out of cash in April 2005 before another savior could be found. Two Chinese companies bought a variety of rights to existing models and programs (meantime squabbling over who had bought what, and when), a development company secured the actual land on which the Longbridge buildings were placed, and all manner of unsavory wrangles then developed. Automobiles that had gone

out of production in 2005 staggered back into life in China, under different names, but even three years on, the Longbridge plant was still un-used. After that, BMW gritted its corporate teeth and wondered if any of that multi-million dollar loan would ever be re-paid…

Mini, or MINI? What's in a name?

Of all the problems inherited by BMW, that of designing, engineering, and bringing a new-generation Mini to market provided the single lasting success that came out of it all. By any standards, the six years it took to get "Good Idea" to "Showroom" was worth it.

When BMW bought the Rover Group in 1994, the assets

As in body building plants throughout the BMW empire, a positive forest of welding and handling robots dealt with Range Rover body assembly at Solihull.

The massive new-model Range Rover of the 2000s, as engineered under BMW control in the late 1990s, was built using the same rotating sling system as found in other BMW car factories of the period.

BELOW

Rover's Solihull factory had started life as a low-rise government-sponsored "shadow" factory in 1940, where aero-engines had been made. By the 1990s it had been modernized, and was bursting at the seams, to build many varieties of 4x4s, including the Land Rover Discovery. These cars were on their way to tackle the Camel Trophy Challenge in 1995.

included the Mini brand, which, in spite of its ancient heritage, still existed. The legendary Issigonis-designed automobile, all ten feet of cheeky character and amazing packaging for four people, might already have been 35 years old, but it was still in production at Longbridge. The problem, however, was that few Rover staff still believed in Mini, and it was only kept on the market as a way of spreading the financial overheads. An automobile that had sold at the rate of 300,000 automobiles a year in the 1970s had now shrunk to a 20,000-a-year irrelevance, and there were no concrete plans either to update or to replace it completely.

BMW, on the other hand, could see the value of the brand, and were shocked to discover so much apathy about it within Rover. They soon instructed that an all-new model be developed. BMW's target of having the new Mini on sale by 1999 proved optimistic due to excessive delays in design and styling approval and sourcing a suitable engine. However, as far as Longbridge was concerned a new-generation Mini would come first, and an all-new medium-sized automobile (coded R30 for many long and frustrating months) would follow it two or even three years later.

Rover—whose concept engineering team were very accomplished, even though they had been continuously starved of resources and backing—were given responsibility, and an automobile coded R50 rapidly took shape. Design/styling began in 1995 (both Rover, at Gaydon, and BMW, back in Munich, offered alternative schemes, and competitive viewing had to take shape before a particular style was chosen), Longbridge-based engineering followed in 1996, and the first Fiat-powered "skin" prototypes were completed in 1997. At this time the major problem was that BMW needed to find a suitable engine, for neither Rover nor BMW had a suitably small, powerful and environmentally "clean" power unit for such a small automobile. In the end the company had to look outside its boundaries for assistance. After a rather frantic search, power eventually came from a gasoline engine jointly-developed with Chrysler. When it finally got under way, manufacture would be in Brazil, and delivery of mass-production quantities would be by ship. The style of the new car would be a three-door hatchback, built around the front-seat "package" dimensions of a BMW 3-Series. A diesel engine, when finalized, was another joint-enterprise, which would eventually come from Toyota. As with the original type, the new Mini was still to be a transverse-engined front-wheel-drive automobile, but every single component was different from the old—not even the badges were the same, and company publicists eventually called the new automobile the MINI to emphasize the difference. Because it had a new type, trendy and more spacious front seat layout, and had to meet all manner of new safety/crash test laws—the old Mini had always slipped under the barriers due to a number of exemptions granted to ancient automobiles—this was a much larger automobile than before.

Original strategic planning was that the new automobile would be engineered at Longbridge, developed and proven at Gaydon, and then would be manufactured entirely at Longbridge, but this scheme did not survive beyond 1999. At this juncture BMW was tiring of the lack of progress being made by their "English patient," and after sending in a task force of German managers soon took over the day-to-day control of Rover themselves. Then came the announcement of BMW's determination to sell off Rover, either in whole or in part. As one consequence of this "divorce" of March 2000—and it really was as brutal, as traumatic and as financially upsetting as that— BMW elected to retain the MINI project, up-rooting the all-new production machinery that had only recently been installed at Longbridge and transferring it all to Cowley (which they shortly re-christened BMW-Oxford).

Although BMW would then have liked to airbrush out Rover's contribution to the new MINI project, the fact is that this input was considerable. Much of the style, much of the actual engineering, a lot of the testing, and of course a great deal of the DNA, came from the British engineers, though BMW did a superb job of sorting out the rest when it became their responsibility. Sorting out the transfer of new tooling from one factory to another, setting up new production plant, re-establishing the brand, installing fabulous state-of-the art production machinery at Oxford, and selling the new model all over the world was, however, totally to BMW's credit. Not that this could be completed overnight. Although BMW had originally planned to launch the automobile in 2000, it was not until mid-2001 that the first automobiles were delivered. In the beginning, BMW stated that "Plant Oxford" would only build 100,000 MINIs every year, and for a time they could only deliver "One" and Cooper hatchback derivatives, but much more was in the pipeline. In no time, it seemed, a supercharged Cooper S had been added, a Convertible also appeared, a (Toyota) diesel engine became optional, and sales rocketed.

What happened in Oxford in 2000 and 2001 is an ideal business case study—for it was clear that nothing was going to deter BMW from re-shaping the plant, and the image of MINI, in their own image. The factory alongside the dual carriageway to the southeast of Oxford, henceforth to be known as BMW Plant Oxford, was the MINI's new home. Even after re-

development was complete, the buildings were not all as modern as a typical European BMW complex, for this site had all started as a new Pressed Steel Co. Ltd. body plant in the 1920s. BMW had spent a fortune there launching the new Rover 75. Then, in the aftermath to the "divorce," Phoenix agreed to take over the manufacture of the Rover 75—but at Longbridge—while BMW decided that the new MINI should be produced at Oxford. To achieve this, two distinctly different operations had to be carried out almost simultaneously. An entire body-in-white production facility and final assembly line for the new MINI had to be moved 70 miles/113 kilometers to the south, while the already-in-production Rover 75 facilities had to be moved in the other direction. For nine months, this meant that no automobiles were being built at Oxford. BMW spent £230 million (about $400 million) on the changeover. In addition, the existing modern paint shop at Oxford, they said, had cost £80 million (about $136 million) to get ready for the Rover 75 in 1997/1998.

As Plant Director Dr. Diess recalled when the MINI was finally launched: "We had to start by reshaping the building areas, because there was going to be a different way of building the shells, we needed pits and access in different areas, and we

No sooner had BMW absorbed the Rover Group, than they set out to transform, and expand, the range of Land Rovers. This was the first all-new type, the Freelander of 1997, which used Rover gasoline and diesel engines in a very capable 4x4 package. BMW's 2-liter diesel engine would be fitted from 2000.

needed to make allowances for future versions, that I can't tell you about." (This, I now know, was a veiled reference to the Convertible, and Clubman types, which went on sale in subsequent years.)

For a time, at Oxford, it seemed that there was more devastation involved than re-birth. This was a time when entire redundant buildings were flattened by the bulldozers, to make way for what would surely follow in the early 2000s. Even at the end of 2001, for instance, massive factory buildings (old, but extensively modernized in the 1990s), which had been used to assemble Rover 600 body shells, were still being razed.

"We had to clean up the whole area." Dr. Diess told me, "As the last 75 moved through the factory, the contractors followed it. We needed to change a lot of the plant, for the MINI was going to take up more space than the 75 had done."

For months, the Oxford factory was the home of BMW planners and factory construction specialists, the bulldozers, the diggers and the men with the hard hats—but not of a workforce assembling automobiles. Work had to be found for the

In the 1990s, as in so many previous decades, traditionally-engineered Land Rover Defenders had been put together by labor-intensive methods, and came in all manner of types.

RIGHT
With sales of fewer than 30,000 4x4s a year, and with a design which had changed little in a complete generation, Defenders were put together in a leisurely manner at Solihull.

workforce—and some spent time working in other BMW factories. 300 people went to Germany for a time, and up to 100 went to Spartanburg in the USA.

By September 2000 the body-in-white facilities for the new MINI were being installed at Oxford (many pressings and sub-assemblies would come from the Swindon body plant, and from Land Rover at Solihull—a rather messy arrangement that would persist until the late 2000s). The first few pre-production automobiles were built in January 2001, but it was April 2001 before true volume production could begin. All in all, the new Oxford plant would be able to produce up to 100,000 MINIs a year (more when a three-shift operation was introduced). Early in 2001, when the job was finally done, BMW-Oxford had been re-created, as a MINI-only assembly plant. Able to build one automobile every 100 seconds at first, the ultimate capacity was limited only by what the paint shop could handle. Once volume production began in April—first at 25 automobiles a day, then 100, and (by mid-summer) 300—the workforce expanded to suit.

In the meantime, there were two further "pipelines" to be established—one for the supply of engines, the other for front-wheel-drive transmissions. In a joint project with Chrysler (an enterprise that would last only until 2007), production of the all-new "Pentagon" engine was located at Tritec Motors Ltda, at Campo Largo, near Curitiba, in Brazil. It began in series in mid-2000, though the first engine of all had been completed as early as September 1999. Five-speed (Rover-type) gearboxes, which Rover had christened R65, were still to be manufactured in a corner of the Rover complex at Longbridge (that part of the factory would soon be partitioned off from the remainder of the plant), and would be sent to Oxford by the truckload.

As Dr. Diess told me in 2001: "We could still add more buildings if we wanted. The whole site is 850,000 square meters [more than 9 million square feet, which means that only half of it is built over], the right size for building 100,000 to 200,000 automobiles every year. But the tidy-up business will be 80 percent finished by the end of 2001, and we will be in good shape by the end of 2002."

And so it was. As the statistics now show, BMW was soon producing up to 250,000 MINIs a year, a new range was progressively introduced in 2006/2007, gearboxes began to flow in from Getrag and ZF (the Rover box was dropped), and a brand-new engine began its career at Ham's Hall in Birmingham. By mid-2005, the 500,000th new-generation MINI had been built, production was edging up towards 4,000 automobiles every week, and the success of the project looked assured. A

second-generation range appeared in 2006 (in styling terms, few could tell the difference between the original automobile, and this new type), then new-generation engines, engineered jointly with Peugeot of France, but manufactured at Ham's Hall (see Chapter 13), and by 2008 more than a million automobiles had been produced at Oxford, where factory capacity had been squeezed up to at least 250,000 automobiles a year.

Was there more to come? Would BMW add other dormant brands (Triumph, for instance) to the range? Would extra and more extreme derivatives make their appearance? Though BMW assured everyone that the MINI was a unique project, and that it had no intention of introducing other front-wheel-drive automobiles, rumors persisted that other such automobiles might follow after the second generation models appeared, and after a four-wheel-drive SAV model went on sale in 2009.

Land Rover—a missed opportunity

It's a measure of BMW's interest in Land Rover, and its four-wheel-drive technology, that in six years—1994 to 2000, when the Germans controlled the destiny of this ultra-British brand—it commissioned two brand-new models, and oversaw the revival of a third. Only the ancient, but sure-selling Defender (which really did look the same as it had always done since 1948) was left alone.

When BMW took over the Rover Group, they couldn't wait to get their hands on Land Rover's treasure trove of models, of four-wheel-drive experience, and of sheer off-road/soft-road know-how. It wasn't just that products like the Discovery were used for everything from working a farm to towing horseboxes, as well as on the school run. The lofty and prestigious Range Rover was still the choice of the wealthy and the discerning, who thought they needed the best four-wheel-drive chassis in the world even though they might never have to face anything more demanding that a slippery parking lot at the local Mall or superstore. By inserting managers and planners at all levels, BMW soon learned what they needed to know about four-wheel-drive. You may be sure that much of what Land Rover already knew was valuable to BMW when the engineering of the big X5 (a true Range Rover competitor, especially in the North American market) was finalized.

The Land Rover factory at Solihull, however, was something else, a real mish-mash of modern, middle-aged and frankly archaic facilities that had been enlarged, patched up, modernized and generally altered-to-taste since Rover had taken it over in 1945 to build private automobiles. Before that, by the way, it

ROVER—WHAT'S IN A NAME?

Before Rover there was British Leyland, before that the British Motor Corporation, and before that … except to pedantic historians such names mean little, but need analyzing to explain why BMW came to be attracted to the Rover Group business. Way back, there were many independent automobile-making concerns in Britain. Austin and Morris were the largest, while Rover was one of the smaller, but prouder, concerns. Leyland, on the other hand, made trucks, many of them among the best in the world.

In the 1950s and 1960s, then, a whole series of mergers took place, which eventually saw the birth of British Leyland. Austin joined hands with Morris in 1952 to form the British Motor Corporation, Leyland rescued Standard-Triumph from bankruptcy in 1961, Rover joined Leyland in 1966, then BMC + Leyland + Jaguar etc. all became British Leyland in 1968. What was known as the "Austin-Morris" division featured vast but ageing plants at Longbridge (Austin) near Birmingham and Cowley (Morris) near Oxford.

Then it all started to go wrong. After financial disaster hit British Leyland in 1975 it had to be taken into state ownership, and it staggered from crisis to crisis thereafter. The Austin-Morris division became Austin-Rover in the early 1980s, and was re-named the Rover Group in the late 1980s. In the meantime, automobiles were separated from trucks in the 1980s, Jaguar was sold off in 1984 (Ford bought it five years later), and what was known as the Rover Group remained.

had been one of the British government's "shadow" factories, built on the edge of a prosperous Birmingham suburb and open for business from 1940, which originally built components for Bristol military aircraft engines. Rover had once built all its automobiles at Solihull, but by 1994 it was a dedicated 4x4 plant. When BMW took over in 1994, the Defender was 46 years old, the Discovery was five years old, and a patrician, second-generation, Range Rover was just about to be launched (after 24 years of the original, by the way...). All had unique transmissions, chassis and bodywork, and although Land Rover made some of their own engines, other power units came from Rover at Longbridge. Land Rover wanted to build a new and smaller model, but needed investment capital and a new assembly hall to make it happen.

As expected, BMW was not impressed by the factory, but loved the model range, and shortly committed many millions to an update. First they approved the building of a new hall on the northern edge of the site—dedicated to a new smaller machine, the Freelander—allied to which was a brand-new paint shop, then they approved a massive new model program. The second-generation Range Rover arrived almost at once, the Freelander came along in 1997, the second-generation Discovery followed in 1998, and then work began on a completely new type of high-tech Range Rover. Plans were laid to fit more and more BMW power plants in future—a new factory at Ham's Hall, just a few miles away, was to provide 4-cylinder gasoline engines, while BMW engines from Germany and Austria were ear-marked for the forthcoming Range Rover. At the same time, dependence on Longbridge for engines was gradually wound down.

Not only that, but the most modern block in the factory, which was now assembling body shells, was further extended to the east, where a simply enormous new multi-action press was installed to stamp out platforms and complete body sides—this press also being intended to send massive pressings to Longbridge for the new-generation MINI, which was under development. While the body assembly facilities were certainly impressive, and the Freelander hall was at least up-to-date, the

Although the assembly line looks bright enough, the Land Rover Defenders being built at Solihull in the 1990s were strictly old-technology, needing many workmen to screw them all together.

old buildings (modified "shadow factory") that accommodated Range Rover, Discovery and Defender were not. The most modern automobile—the Range Rover—had the most money spent on its assembly lines, which nevertheless meandered through the old building, while the Defender, simple and rugged, but definitely low-tech, took shape in the semi-gloom at the back of the same area.

Although BMW had big plans for Land Rover—4-cylinder BMW diesels had already been slotted into the Freelander, new-generation gasoline engines were sure to follow, and an entire section of the Solihull factory, known as "North Block" was set to be rebuilt for new-generation Discovery assembly to take place—by 2000 they had decided to rid themselves completely of their "English patient." After a company "auction," rather embarrassingly carried out in public, Land Rover was sold off to Ford for £1.6 Billion (about $2.8 Billion at the existing rate of exchange), and BMW swiftly and clinically withdrew. Although it takes no part in this story, it is worth recording that, under Ford tutelage, Land Rover went on to greater heights in the next few years, and that the second-generation Freelander was successfully placed in a Ford factory, at Halewood on Merseyside. BMW themselves had little time or interest in seeing what would become of their "English patient," for henceforth they were far too busy building and rebuilding their business all over the world.

LEFT ABOVE
The Rover L-Series was a fine 2-liter turbo-diesel engine, used in Land Rover models, but by the end of the 1990s BMW had begun to re-engineer Land Rover and Rover models to use BMW diesels instead.

ABOVE
When BMW sold the Land Rover business to Ford in 2000, part of its "dowry" was that this all-new third-generation Range Rover was almost ready for production. Designed and developed to BMW's own standards, it was an expensive and luxuriously-equipped SUV, which used BMW engines, and manufacturing expertise.

CHAPTER 12

COVERING A HUGE MARKET— SEDANS, SPORTS CARS, GASOLINE, AND DIESEL

IN THE 1980S AND 1990S, BMW SPENT MUCH TIME building on their established success in Europe, and still found time to become absorbed in several other major expansion schemes. These involved completely new factories or new businesses—one in North America, one in South Africa and another (eventually abortive, as it transpired) in Great Britain. The miracle is that, in spite of all this, new models continued to flow from Germany, and demand for automobiles followed its ever-rising curve towards the million mark.

Less than three years after the very first cars were built at the Regensburg factory, BMW celebrated the assembly of the first 100,000 examples, and chose to add this distinction to a 3-Series Cabriolet.

An appropriate moment to survey the company's progress came in 1982, when the second-generation 5-Series sedans (which looked very similar to the originals, but were vastly different under the skin), and the second-generation 3-Series—always known within the factory as the E30 range—had both appeared. Not only did the 3-Series include a very popular four-door alternative to the existing two-door, but also an aggressive motorsport marketing program was set up, which would soon result in the M3 model taking to the racetracks with huge success.

By the end of 1982, therefore, the BMW product range looked like this:

3-Series—315, 316, 318i, 320i, 323i models, with 4- or 6-cylinder engines, two-door or four-door sedan bodies, all built at Milbertshofen/Munich.
  Certain 3-Series models were also assembled, mainly from kits imported from Germany, at Rosslyn in South Africa.

5-Series—518, 520i, 525i and 528i, with four cylinder or two different types of 6-cylinder engines, and four-door sedan shells, all built at Dingolfing.

Engine assembly at the Munich factory was an increasingly complex, and high-tech, business by the late 1980s. By this time BMW was making four, six, V8 and V12 gasoline engines.

6-Series—628CSi, 633CSi and 635 CSi, with 6-cylinder engines and two-door coupe body shells, all built at Dingolfing.

7-Series—728i, 732i, 735i and 745i, all with 6-cylinder engines (the 745i being a turbocharged unit), all built at Dingolfing.

In addition, 7-Series automobiles and original-series 5-Series automobiles were being built at Rosslyn in South Africa. This, too, was the moment when the new engine-building plant at Steyr, in Austria, was coming on stream.

The next major change in Munich was to move the secret design and development departments out of the old Milbertshofen complex to brand new buildings that were erected in Knorrstrasse, just a few city blocks to the north. Not only did BMW need more space in which to develop its ever-expanding list of new models, but it also needed more security from "spy cameras" than it enjoyed at Milbertshofen. Need I say that although the new complex was built with generous allowances for expansion, by the early 2000s it, too, was bursting at the seams—one consequence being that the MINI project had to take shape in yet another group of new buildings. By the early 2000s, indeed, Munich was even more of a "one business" city that it had ever previously been.

From 1983, therefore, there was an opportunity to rationalize, expand and modernize the Milbertshofen plant for what felt like the umpteenth time. Once a thorough modernization program had been completed, with D & D moved out and with Steyr taking on more and more aspects of engine manufacture, the manufacture of large new tools could also be dispersed. Plans were also laid for the relocation of the foundry, which would eventually hand over all its work to a much-modernized ex-Glas plant at Landshut, half way between Munich and Dingolfing.

Because Steyr gradually took over more and more manufacture of what I might flippantly call the "mass-production" BMW engines—4-cylinder gasoline, 6-cylinder gasoline and diesel power units—serious thought could finally be given to the finalization of two exciting new engine product lines. They were entirely unrelated 90-degree V8 and 60-degree V12 gasoline units, which the BMW engineers had been dabbling with for some time. Along with the super-high-performance M-Type (M = motorsport, of course) versions of 4-cylinder and 6-cylinder engines (for M3, M5 and M6 production automobiles), these needed more space so that they could be built at a more leisurely and even more dedicated pace. this was found in what was known as Hall 140. To put this major development into context, the very first V12-engined BMW—the 300bhp/5.0-liter 750i sedan—was put on sale at the end of 1986, while the new-generation V8 (the M60, which was absolutely no relation to the old design used in automobiles like the 507 of the 1950s) followed on in 1992.

By this time, it is certainly worth noting, BMW was producing a bewildering variety of gasoline engines in Munich—growing numbers of the more modern "M20 small six" cylinder types, the old M30 6-cylinder types (which would eventually be stretched to 3.8-liters), the new M60 V8s and the M70 V12s. If the engineers and (most definitely) the hundreds of "petrol heads" who joined the company at this time, had got their way, they would have introduced even more. Anyone lucky enough to visit the BMW Classic departments, and be allowed to look at their private museum, would see a range of

"might-have-been" prototypes, including V6 types intended for mass-production, V10s that might have been fitted to F1 automobiles years before such configurations became fashionable, while there was even time for a V16 version of the V12 to be built and installed (just—it was a tight squeeze) in a 7-Series of the period.

All of this added to the demands on space that were regularly made on the Milbertshofen plant to fulfill the worldwide demand for 3-Series automobiles—which were still being made, exclusively, at this plant. The result was that more and more peripheral operations (tool rooms and repair facilities among them), had to be moved out. In the end, though, the directors had to make the first of the many billion-Deutschmark decisions that would be made in the 1980s and 1990s—that a third assembly plant was going to be needed—and soon.

ABOVE
To allow them to make many more 3-Series cars than before, BMW opened up a new plant at Regensburg, north-east of Munich, in 1986.

Time marches on—after a phenomenally long career, assembly of Type E30 3-Series cars finally came to an end at Milbertshofen in 1990. A new-generation of 3-Series was soon to take its place.

By the 1990s Regensburg had become the third major German assembly plant for BMWs, and would concentrate on 1-Series and 3-Series derivatives in the 2000s.

Regensburg—a third assembly plant

By the mid-1980s, the sales trend of BMWs was still resolutely pointing upwards, and the company was quite confident that it would soon run out of space in Munich and at Dingolfing. Accordingly, another nationwide search began to locate a site for a third Germany assembly plant.

Ideally, of course, the company would have liked to make the existing plants even bigger than they already were, but this was not considered possible (certainly not at Munich where the expansion of buildings had reached the border of every public road surrounding the site long ago). It was also not practical at Dingolfing, as much of that plant was still surrounded by rolling farmland that BMW did not then own. So, what to do, and where to do it? As with the development and the modernization of Dingolfing, BMW wanted to keep its new, third, plant as close to Munich as was reasonably possible—though not so close that establishing it would "poach" production staff from the

established plants. In the end the planners settled on the city of Regensburg, in Lower Bavaria, which was only 20 miles/32 kilometers further north of Dingolfing and the massive BMW foundry at Landshut, and that much more remote from Munich itself. Two major autobahns—the Munich to Dresden, and Frankfurt to Vienna highways—crossed each other at the outskirts of Regensburg, which meant that the transport links with the rest of Germany were ideal, while Siemens (the major automotive electronic supplier) already had a presence in the city.

Having secured a site in 1982, BMW then set about building a brand-new manufacturing plant, which completed its first automobiles—3-Series sedans—in 1986. At first Regensburg was little more than an assembly plant of components that were mostly shipped in from other sites (notably Munich and Steyr), but it was rapidly built up to tackle much more manufacturing of its own. The paint shop for body shells was opened in 1987, body shells themselves were assembled and manufactured from

1990, while the press shop itself was completed in 1997; this made Regensburg at least as self-sufficient as other BMW facilities. By the 2000s, Regensburg had become a partner of equal importance to other, older (and more established) BMW sites. At first it concentrated on building 3-Series sedans, but other derivatives (including the stub-tailed 3-Series Compact) soon followed and, as we will see in Chapter 12, it also became a vital part of the entire 1-Series production network, and of convertibles in general. Regensburg, in fact, became the centre of BMW convertible/Cabriolet assembly, for which top management awarded it their rating as the "center of competence."

Special products
While BMW was moving steadily into the building of more and yet more special sporty models (M3 and M5 automobiles in particular), those outside the company assumed that such automobiles could be produced easily, by dove-tailing them with the more normal types—but this was far from the truth. The two-door M3 sedan of 1986, for instance, might have looked superficially similar to other 3-Series types, but at that time it was the only automobile in the range to be fitted with a twin-overhead-camshaft 16-valve version of the 4-cylinder engine, while the body shell (which included flared front and rear wing pressings, and a different roof/rear glass profile) was also

As BMW's annual sales soared well above half-a-million cars a year, the demand for engines was immense. Steyr came in for continuous expansion, with Phase V well under way in May 1996.

Even in modern times, some seam welding, by hand, still takes place.

different in many subtle ways. To accommodate these automobiles, and others that followed, BMW somehow found space to set up dedicated departments and assembly facilities within the Munich/Milbertshofen plant itself. The launch of the very first of BMW's Z-sports automobiles—the Z1—was a perfect case in point, as was the way that the M1 Supercar (see the panel on page 103) was given its final look-over in Munich after Baur of Stuttgart had completed the manufacture.

By the mid-1980s, BMW had been out of the sports car market for decades, and was not at all sure that it should ever try to re-enter that specialized field. In a typically cautious way,

therefore, the Z1 project was a fascinating toe-in-the water exercise, and there is no doubt that what was learned from it was all valuable when BMW came to produce the Z3 roadster at Spartanburg in the mid-1990s. Z1, incidentally, was an acronym for *Zentral Entwicklung No.1* (Central Development Project No.1), which was a specialized new department within the ever-growing BMW operation. The Z1 was never meant to sell in big numbers over a lengthy period—in fact, exactly 8,000 such two-seaters would be produced between 1988 and 1991—but it demonstrated that BMW was quite capable of designing, developing and building any type of private automobile. (The

Within ten years of its establishment in the late 1980s, the Regensburg factory was already beginning to fill up all available ground space—and a fourth assembly plant, at Leipzig, was becoming necessary.

other type of automobile that BMW had not so far attempted to sell was in the big four-wheel-drive market, though, as will become very clear in the final chapter, such machines were already in the mind of corporate planners for production in the 2000s...)

Although the style and engineering of the BMW Z1 were conventional enough, the construction was anything but. The new automobile was based on the platform and running gear of the latest BMW 3-Series range, and used a 170bhp/2,494cc version of the "small six" cylinder engine, this being married to an entirely new type of multi-link/coil spring/independent rear suspension (colloquially known within and without BMW as the "Z-axle")—a layout that eventually became standardized in

ABOVE

Exactly 8.000 of the two-seater BMW Z1 (Z standing for Zentral Entwicklung, meaning Central Development Project) were produced by the factory between 1988 and 1991.

RIGHT

Even in a highly automated factory, there was still time for a little bit of careful hand-work, this being the hand-stitching of the leather cover to a steering wheel, at Munich.

FAR RIGHT

What BMW enthusiasts call the "small six" cylinder engine was first introduced in the late 1970s, and was still being manufactured in Munich in the late-2000s. Pistons and connecting rods are being added to the assembly at this stage.

many other BMW (and MINI) models.

The bodywork, however, was novel in so many ways. Not only did this feature exterior bolt-on panels in Xenoy, a high-tech thermoplastic, but the two doors were arranged, not to swing open, or even to swing upwards, but to retract

downwards into recesses in the body sills, which were both high and capacious. It was perfectly feasible to drive the automobiles with those doors retracted (and in warm climates many owners did so), even though the passengers' bodies were exposed to view from onlookers. For this reason the Z1 could never be sold in

This pressing makes up the inside of the bonnet panel on a modern BMW 7-Series model, and is being moved from station to station by robots.

Careful hand work, including the fitment of seats, the center console, and checking out the safety belt positions.

FAR RIGHT
BMW's body assembly department in Munich is a highly automated process, with all weld-operations being carried out by calibrated machines.

BELOW
The start of it all ! Rolls of steel have been delivered from the suppliers, and will soon be turned into complex pressings in the Press Shop in Munich.

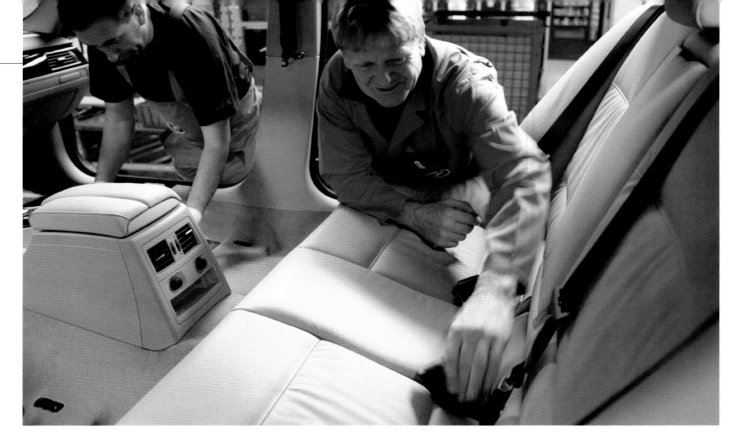

the United States—there seemed to be many Federal safety regulations that it could not satisfy. Because the Z1 used many new materials, new constructional details, and new manufacturing techniques, it was always bound to be an expensive automobile. When put on sale in 1988 it cost 85,000 German Deutschmarks, which (at the exchange rates of the day) was about £26,500 (around $48,000) and put it close to the elite levels of Porsche pricing.

Although Z1 was always intended to be built in Munich/Milbertshofen it was kept well clear of the main 3-Series assembly lines, which were already producing 1,000 automobiles every day. Z1 assembly, on the other hand, was never likely to exceed more than 15 automobiles a day. Once the assembly process had settled down, the cycle time (the interval between successive automobiles reaching the same state of assembly) had been reduced to 36 minutes (slightly less than two automobiles every working hour if everything went well), which would have made any Detroit employee die of boredom. To meet production requirements, BMW re-equipped what had previously been the "pilot plant" (the section of the business that had been used to build pre-production, or what was sometimes known as "shakedown" automobiles.) The pilot plant moved to the new Research and Innovation Center in 1986. The production area in Hall 159, of only 2,800 square meters (or 30,120 square feet) was actually spread over three levels and was therefore small, compact, and reasonably secure, with a total workforce of only 130 employees.

Although Hall 159 only contained Z1 assembly for three years, it would later be turned over to producing BMW special vehicles of many types—where the numbers involved were not high, but where the complexity of extra added equipment was considerable. The completion of automobiles for the German Federal police authorities was a perfect example of the challenges, and the solutions, which Hall 159 came to tackle.

The colossus gets bigger

BMW themselves could always provide one easy way of measuring the breadth, and weight, of their product range in the mid-1990s, which was to know just how many engines were needed in any one year. At the end of 1996, when the decision was made to build a brand-new engine manufacturing plant at Ham's Hall near Birmingham in Great Britain (I describe this in more detail in the final chapter), the company

Modern BMW sedans use massive one-piece pressings, to ensure the quality of assembly—this single stamping including the entire body side panel of a 7-Series.

circulated a list of the engines that it was already producing in a year:

Plant	Engine and Capacity	Number Built in a Year
Munich	V8 3.0/3.5/4.0/4.4-liter	50,000
	V12 5.4/5.6-liter	10,000
	Straight-six 2.0/ 2.5/2.8/3.0/3.2-liter	222,000
Steyr	Gasoline—4-cyl 1.6/1.8-liter	227,000
(Austria)	Diesel—4-cyl 1.7-liter	35,000
	Diesel—6-cyl 2.5-liter	67,700
Grand Total (in 1995)		611,700

This, please note, was before the great surge in sales of diesel-engined BMWs took place, and was before supplies to the Rover Group even started. This had all come about by the gradual renewal of several model ranges, by the addition of several new different derivatives, and by the constant building/rebuilding battles that were regularly carried out at Munich, Dingolfing and Regensburg to increase the production capacity of the plants.

As the 1980s gave way to the 1990s, the biggest launch of all was of the new-generation 3-Series (BMW staff always knew it as the E36 range), for Munich and Regensburg had to be extensively equipped to cope with its new features. Perhaps the best way to summarize what was going on in so many places is to summarize the BMW product range in 1992, just ten years after the summary provided earlier in this chapter:

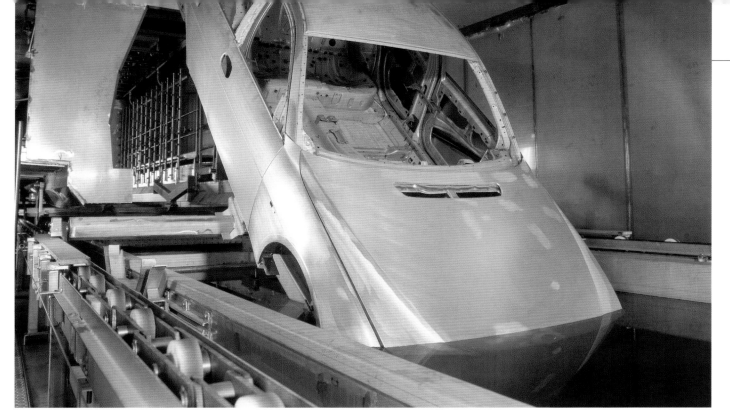

LEFT
The paint shop procedure at any one of BMW's manufacturing plants is similar. Here, a big sedan shell is on its way to one of the pre-paint, corrosion-proofing dip tanks ....

BELOW LEFT
.... a process in which the entire shell is completely somersaulted so that no section is missed.

BELOW
After the pre-paint dip was completed, the shell was thoroughly drained before going on to the next station.

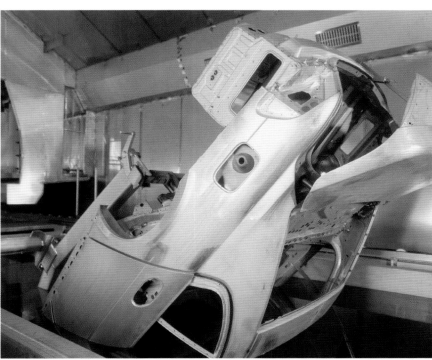

3-Series: 316i to 325i, in sedan, coupe, Touring (estate) and Cabriolet guise, with gasoline or diesel engines, assembled at Munich/Milbertshofen, Regensburg and Rosslyn (South Africa). Ultra-high performance M3 types also in production. First announced in **late 1990**, and new versions regularly being launched.

5-Series: 518i to 540i, in sedan and Touring guide, with 4-cylinder, 6-cylinder gasoline and diesel engines, and 4-liter V8 gasoline engines, all assembled at Dingolfing. Ultra-high performance M5 types also in production. First announced in **January 1988.**

7-Series: 730i to 750i, all sedans in standard or longer-wheelbase form, with 6-cylinder, V8 and V12 gasoline engines, all assembled at Dingolfing. First announced in **Autumn 1986.**

8-Series: 840i to 850CSi, all 2+2 Coupes, with V8 or V12 gasoline engines, all assembled at Dingolfing. First announced in **September 1989.**

In recent years, therefore, there had been a succession of new-model launches for automobiles to be built at Dingolfing—5-Series, 7-Series and 8-Series—but at least this plant had been laid out in the 1970s with a great deal of scope built in for further expansion, and with the possibility of more land being acquired alongside the new and modern buildings. Munich/Milbertshofen, however, could expand no further outwards—to the north, south, east and west, public highways made that impossible—and there was no industrial justification in trying to grow it upwards. The only possibility—and it was one in which billions of Deutschmarks had already been spent, and would further be spent in the future—was for the interior facilities to be comprehensively up-dated.

Modernizing in Munich

In the 1980s and 1990s, Munich/Milbertshofen seemed to be in a constant state of flux. With much work completed ahead of the launch of the E30 3-Series range, and much more to be done to cope with new derivatives in the 1990s, contractors' vehicles were constantly on the premises. Now it can be revealed that, in the early 1990s, BMW seriously considered the possibility that it might stop modernizing the space-bound Munich plant completely, in favor of concentrating its efforts on the expansion of Dingolfing, Regensburg, Steyr and (soon) the Spartanburg

factories instead. At one time, there was a proposal that Milbertshofen should close down by 2000. But was this wise? How would it affect the company's overall profitability? Was it likely that too many assumptions would be made about future growth? And what would the captive workforce in Munich think of all this? All in all, though, it never seemed to be a compelling proposal, and would soon be discarded.

The fact of the matter was that in the 1990s demand for 3-Series automobiles was so high, and apparently growing steadily, that BMW needed every assembly line that it could find. At Munich, an early step in the 1980/1990s was comprehensive modernization of the paint plant, and during the 1990s the final dismantlement of the old foundry allowed even more paint lines to be installed. At Milbertshofen, as at so many factories all over the world, the "pinch point" in the assembly process was in the paint shop, and any increase in capacity was welcome. There was an all-new paint shop from 2003. Not only that, but the decision was taken that all of BMW's V-layout gasoline engines—V8s and V12s—should continue to be manufactured at Milbertshofen, along with the "small six" engines (though, in truth, the largest of those "small" sixes now displaced 3.2-liters/195CID).

The truly major change, which was phased in by 1997/1998 when the fourth-generation 3-Series (the E46 range) took over from the E36, was that a single-line assembly principle should be adopted: all models, of all bodies—no matter what their different engines, equipment or features—should be built down

Secure in its rotating cradle, this is how assembly of modern BMWs was made easier for the workforce.

OPPOSITE

In a modern factory, the use of complex and versatile robots—for welding, for jigging, and for transportation of panels from place to place, is quite essential.

the same line. Even before then, one major change, which eased the backbreaking toil of some operations, was that a tilting assembly system (which had already been trialed at Regensburg) was also installed in Munich. This meant that structures suitably supported in cradles could be tilted through 90 degrees, as if on a spit, so that work on the underside of the shells could more easily be carried out. This was all part of a constant re-appraisal of the Munich plant, what it could achieve, and how it might be enlarged "by stealth" in the future.

Z8—in structural aluminum

Not that BMW only busied itself with the making of family automobiles. Looking back there was the Z8 Roadster, which brightened the company's image in the early 2000s. It is easy enough to brand the extrovert Z8 Roadster as a marketing failure, though this judgment may be harsh. Although total sales of just 5,703 two-seaters in four years was small by BMW standards, the Z8 was the first corporate automobile to bring aluminum frame technology and series production together— and it provided invaluable experience for the design and building of the first BMW-owned Rolls-Royce model (the Phantom) which followed. Here was another automobile which might be seen as an indulgence, the sort that could only ever be put on sale by a company (like BMW) that was experiencing long-term and quite incredible demand for all its products. The engineering, the marketing, the publicity and the positive public relations images to be gained from such a machine was considered more important than the loss-making financial performance.

And loss-making, if BMW ever admitted to it, the Z8 certainly was. The story goes that two of BMW's most extrovert bosses—Wolfgang Reitzle and Bernd Pischetsrieder—were once inspecting a 1950s-style 507 at a company celebration, decided that they really ought to do something like that again, and suggested that the company's Californian-based Designworks offices might work up a concept. The result was the V8-engined ZO7 concept, which first appeared at the Tokyo Motor Show in 1997. A production automobile, the Z8, speedily followed it through the development process, and was duly put into production in the same Hall 159 at Milbertshofen in which the Z1 had been built ten years earlier.

The Z8, however, was not merely important because of its extrovert style and performance (or, indeed, for its starring role in the James Bond film The World is Not Enough), but for its construction. For some years BMW had been looking to save

weight in its new models—every time a new model came along, it tended to be larger and heavier then before, partly because essential new safety features such as multiple airbags and body-shell reinforcements had to be included—and one way, they concluded, was to use aluminum instead of steel and cast iron in the automobiles' structures. Like iron, aluminum was a very plentiful metal, but pound for pound it was also more expensive. For BMW this meant squaring the circle, but paring weight out of components by using aluminum rather than steel became an obsession, and even today we have not seen the final result of the pioneering work that went ahead.

For the Z8, therefore, BMW evolved a complex new chassis, which proved to be an advanced type of welded and extruded aluminum space frame construction, equally as stiff as a steel frame would have been, but lighter. There was space for it to be somewhat bulkier than the equivalent steel frame might have been, but in a two-seater roadster this was not a critical problem. To keep the faith as far as weight reduction was concerned, much of the body shell was also made up of pressed or fabricated aluminum panels, which were riveted, welded and bonded together.

Because the first fruits of aluminum instead of steel technology had been employed at Dingolfing, in 5-Series, 7-Series and 8-Series models, what BMW rather proudly dubbed the "aluminum center of competence" was based at Dingolfing. The center was housed there in a separate building and part of the complex, where much of the development took place. However, when the time came to build the production automobiles, Hall 159 at Milbertshofen served a useful purpose once again—this time with about 100 specially trained employees, and a cycle time of 50 minutes. As with the Z1, there was no moving assembly line: the part-built automobiles were pushed gently from station to station when the time was appropriate.

Looking to the new century

When the twentieth century finally came to an end, BMW seemed to have made all the decisions that would shape the organization in the next decade and more. The Rover/Land Rover "experiment" was to be discarded. The MINI project was close to maturity. New plants at Spartanburg and Ham's Hall were coming to fruition. Yet another assembly plant (it would be placed at Leipzig) was being considered. An all-new product line (the 1-Series) was already under development. There was much to challenge the company in the years to come.

MULTI-NATIONAL COLOSSUS

◀ MO 020 L

Assembly

157

CHAPTER 13

MILLION-PLUS PRODUCTION IN FIVE CONTINENTS

BY THE END OF THE FIRST DECADE IN THE TWENTY-FIRST CENTURY, BMW's annual global output of automobiles was reaching toward the 1.5 million level, and the company's public ambition was to breach the 2 million mark. Expansion, and the development of new facilities was so intense in those years that what follows in this chapter can be no more than a snapshot of the "story so far." So much change took place, in so many different locations, that they have had to be compartmentalized to make a complex story understandable.

To summarize, by the end of that first decade, BMW controlled no fewer than 23 production plants in 12 countries. Of these, 14 assembled BMW automobiles, but we must not forget three other important sites—Oxford, England, where MINIs were produced, Goodwood, England where Rolls-Royce automobiles were assembled, and Berlin, where the building of motorcycles had been located since 1969. All in all, there was production in Europe, the United States, assembly on several sites in southeast Asia, and manufacture in South Africa. Production of engines (for MINIs) in Brazil had just ended, but there were opportunities for expansion in many other countries and locations.

Although this might look like a typical BMW factory in Europe, it is in fact a assembly plant in Thailand, which accepts CKD packs from Europe, and completes 3-Series for its own, and geographically close, markets.

By the 2000s, BMW was truly a world-wide operation, with manufacturing plants in Germany, Britain, the USA and South America, and assembly plants in many other locations.

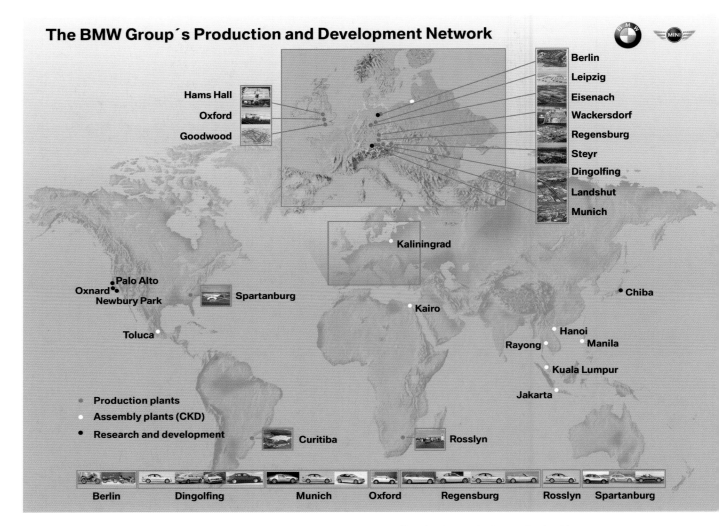

The BMW Group´s Production and Development Network

Hams Hall
Oxford
Goodwood

Berlin
Leipzig
Eisenach
Wackersdorf
Regensburg
Steyr
Dingolfing
Landshut
Munich

Kaliningrad

Palo Alto
Oxnard
Newbury Park

Spartanburg

Chiba

Kairo

Toluca

Hanoi
Rayong
Manila

Kuala Lumpur

Jakarta

• Production plants
○ Assembly plants (CKD)
● Research and development

Curitiba

Rosslyn

Berlin   Dingolfing   Munich   Oxford   Regensburg   Rosslyn   Spartanburg

Back into East Germany

No sooner had the Berlin Wall come down at the end of 1989, and the Iron Curtain dissolved, than the re-unification of Germany took place. After the collapse of communism, a nation divided in 1945 could finally look forward to coming together again. Like many other industrial giants, BMW accepted the fact that it would never be recompensed for the annexation of its business, but saw that there were big opportunities for moving back into the eastern part of the nation where the infrastructure was in disarray, and which had suffered grievously from a lack of investment.

Only months after re-unification was announced, in July 1990, BMW saw that the Eisenach business—which was building dreadful little Wartburg automobiles—was about to die, so they moved back towards the town and set about commissioning a new factory close by. Although there was no intention of trying to rejuvenate the old plant, nor to assemble complete BMW automobiles and motorcycles, it was decided to set up a modern tool-making operation, which would craft press tools for the stamping out of major pressings like doors, fenders and roof panels. When it opened up in March 1992,

The BMW test center at Nurburgring where new model prototypes are rigorously tested.

Little spare space here at Leipzig, as painted 3-Series body shells await their turn to join the final assembly lines.

The Leipzig plant was the fourth major BMW car-assembly plant to be opened up in Germany. Industry watchers will see that there was still much available space for expansion after the first phase had been completed.

When the Leipzig assembly plant opened up in the early 2000s, it was BMW's latest, and most modern, car plant.

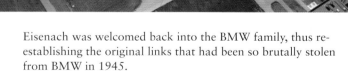

Eisenach was welcomed back into the BMW family, thus re-establishing the original links that had been so brutally stolen from BMW in 1945.

Even bigger plans, though, were laid for Leipzig, a city quite new to BMW. Once ruined by Allied bombing, it had been patched up by the Communist regime of East Germany and was a city desperately in need of investment and modernization. Although BMW had never before operated from this German city, which was a long way north of Munich, but southwest of Berlin, in Saxony, an attractive series of financial offers from the local government caused the company to set up a big new assembly plant there. At the same time, incidentally, Porsche also set up shop in this city, though the two enterprises were not linked. Like Regensburg and Dingolfing before it, the Leipzig plant was meant to operate as a mirror-image plant to home turf in Munich. Finally coming on stream in March 2005, it was meant to employ up to 5,500 workers, and to build up to 650 automobiles every day—that's more than 150,000 units a year—and to emphasize that this was possible, the new factory clocked up 50,000 automobiles before the end of the calendar year.

Inevitably, the first Leipzig products were the latest-model 3-Series sedans, for which there seemed to be an inexhaustible demand, but this was only a start. The first 100,000 marker was laid down in February 2006, manufacture of three-door 1-Series sedans followed in 2007, and a third-model, the 1-Series Coupe, followed in July 2007. A fourth model—the 1-Series Convertible—was also added to the line-up at the end of 2007, by which time the plant employed 5,000 workers. It was clear that Leipzig, like Regensburg had been since the 1990s, was already becoming a cornerstone of BMW's long-term expansion.

The Austrian connection

As I have already made clear, by the 1990s the modern factory at Steyr, in Austria, had become the company's largest engine production plant, and was at the center of all diesel-engine production. This plant, which had expanded mightily in recent years, was totally bound up in engine production, as well as supplying myriads of engine components to other engine plants in Munich, and at Ham's Hall in England.

From 2003, however, another Austrian enterprise became linked with BMW, for a new BMW product line—the four-wheel-drive X3 "SAV" (Sports Activity Vehicle)—had to find a home. However, and I have emphasized this several times in earlier sections, because of the ever-growing popularity of other models, this new automobile could not be accommodated in any existing BMW plant. While it might have made some sense to build X3s alongside X5s, this would have meant locating the X3 in Spartanburg, USA, which BMW did not want to do at that stage.

It was time for another European-wide search, and in the end, BMW settled on a specialist independent plant—Magna Steyr in Graz, Austria. Here was not only a company with a large, distinguished and ever-growing list of clients, but one that had also been involved in the development of the new X3's four-wheel-drive installation. Although the first automobiles had been previewed in the press during 2003, volume production began in Graz early in 2004, and before long there was a three-shift

Final adjustments to a newly-assembly BMW 3-Series at the Leipzig factory.

Checking that a new car can be as quite as possible in all details—this is one of BMW's acoustic test chambers.

assembly process in operation, with up to 400 automobiles a day being produced.

Rosslyn, South Africa

By the end of the twentieth century, the South African factory at Rosslyn was a fully-fledged assembly plant for 3-Series models. The greater part of those automobiles was manufactured on the site (though major mechanical items like engine and transmissions were shipped in from Europe). BMW had just invested a billion Rand (about $100 to $120 million, depending on the exchange rate of the period), and in 1998 the latest 3-Series (the E46 type) had gone into production on the site.

By 2000, Rosslyn was assembling 170 3-Series automobiles a day, which was more than enough to satisfy its home market and resulted in exports to other continents—including delivery to British and German customers. Rosslyn-built 3-Series automobiles were delivered to the United States from 2000 onward, more than 55,000 units were built in 2002 alone, and before E46 assembly ended in 2005 no fewer than 269,810 such 3-Series types had been assembled in South Africa. As with BMW's other plants, worldwide, Rosslyn had ambitions to become larger, and to build even more automobiles. This was emphasized when the latest 3-Series—the new E60 type—went into production in South Africa in 2005.

Ham's Hall

BMW's ability to turn a corporate setback into a great asset was proved, emphatically, by what happened at Ham's Hall, in England, in the 1990s and 2000s. Soon after BMW had absorbed the Rover/Land Rover businesses in 1994, the strategic decision was made to gradually fit BMW engines—gasoline and diesel—to every suitable product in the British range—and to manufacture those engines close to the Rover (Longbridge) and Land Rover (Solihull) assembly plants.

By late 1996, the £400 million (approx $700 million) decision had been made. First of all, BMW found a derelict power station at Ham's Hall, which was due east of Birmingham, and a mere 10 miles/16 kilometers from Solihull, and which was ripe for re-development. They then decided to build up a range of new-type 1.6-liter, 1.8-liter and 2.0-liter 4-cylinder gasoline engines in a brand-new and highly automated factory on that site. These engines would not only service Rover and Land Rover, but would also be used to power 3-Series and (though we did not know it at the time) 1-Series automobiles to

LEFT
Many years ago, factories used to look dirty, and belched much smoke. In the 2000s, though, BMW's new plant at Leipzig was clean, airy, environmentally efficient, and somehow did not look at all 'industrial'.

LEFT
BMW 3-Series body shells wait their turn for completion, at the modern factory in Leipzig.

FACING PAGE
An evocative shot showing a critical point reached thousands of times every day in a modern BMW factory—where the trimmed body shells is "married" to the engine, transmission and suspension assemblies.

LEFT
BMW completely rebuilt the old Rover Group factory in Oxford, England, so that it could become a dedicated MINI manufacturing plant. In this case, a Convertible, supported in a rotary sling, is ahead of sun-roof hatchback model.

RIGHT
BMW's MINI subsidiary built the 500,000th new-generation MINI, at Oxford, England, in August 2004. Within three years, overall Oxford production had already exceeded one million.

The front-wheel-drive MINI was an entirely different type of car from anything previously built by BMW—and was assembled in the dedicated plant at Oxford, England.

be built in Germany. As BMW told us in 1996, Munich's engine output was then 282,000 units, that of Steyr in Austria (which included every diesel) was 330,000 units, while at the same time Rover and Land Rover between them were hoovering up another 500,000 engines for their own use. Capacity, rather than demand, was the usual constraint.

Strategically it all made a great deal of sense—until BMW abruptly decided to rid itself of the Rover/Land Rover business at short notice in 2000. Months before Ham's Hall was due to come on stream (pilot production had already begun), BMW decided to pull out of Great Britain, only keeping the MINI business—which was scheduled to use Brazilian-built engines! One consequence was that instead of being an ideally placed new engine factory, Ham's Hall became a plant that would supply all of its output back to Germany. Fortunately for all concerned, Ham's Hall did not immediately become a "white elephant." Financially, it still made sense for this new plant to come into existence, though its location (close to Rover/Land Rover factories) was no longer an advantage. The rest of the story, indeed, is easily told. From 2001 this highly automated, clean, quiet and efficient plant had begun producing engines in big quantities (70,000 engines in the first year alone, the millionth being reached in 2007), and the published figures show just how much it contributed to the group as the years passed.

There was one major strategic change that helped to rescue Ham's Hall's promise. As already described (in Chapter 11), and detailed once again below, the MINI project became increasingly important to the entire BMW business, and sales continued to increase every year during the 2000s. Unhappily, the Chrysler-designed engine in the original automobiles was not a success, and when the second-generation MINI came along in 2006, a brand-new gasoline engine, jointly developed with PSA (effectively Peugeot-Citroen) took its place. Instead of being manufactured in Brazil, the new engine was to be built in Europe, so Ham's Hall was ideally placed to take on that job. Within months of its introduction in 2006, output at Ham's Hall had virtually doubled, and the plant had become highly profitable.

A few facts and figures re-emphasize just what a vast and global business BMW had become by this time. In 2007, Ham's Hall produced no less than 367,000 gasoline engines (which compared with 216,000 in 2006, and was of course a new record), of which 172,600 went to MINI. Of the 194,400 BMW engines that made up the balance, these were intended for use in 1-Series, 3-Series, 5-Series, Z4 and X3 models, and were destined for delivery to plants in Austria, Germany, South Africa and the USA. The workforce had risen to 1,000 associates, who attended

on a three-shift basis, in a plant that operated in what (to some observers, including the writer) seemed to be an almost uncannily quiet and measured way.

Although it was not yet at capacity (there were forecasts of increased BMW *and* MINI outputs in the future), we have heard this sort of statement before, and the company might soon be faced with what has become a regular investment decision—either increasing the build rate within the existing plant, or of enlarging the plant. Fortunately, at Ham's Hall, BMW had already acquired more land that it originally needed, and could see where and how extra buildings could be added. And in the meantime, the original destiny laid out for Ham's Hall—to supply engines to Rover Group factories nearby—has long been forgotten…

MINI—a growing empire

In Chapter 11 I described how BMW finally extracted itself from the financial morass of the British Rover Group, how it kept control of the MINI brand, and how it brought a new automobile to market in mid-2001. In the years that followed, that very brave decision proved itself time and time again. Although the building of MINIs might not have been as profitable as was a BMW, it was still an operation of which the company was proud, and that continued to grow as the 2000s proceeded.

As with the re-jigging of priorities for the use of the Ham's Hall engine plant, the way in which MINIs were to be manufactured had to be modified after the "divorce" from Rover, and after MINI final assembly was concentrated on Oxford. In the late 1990s, the new MINI was scheduled to be built within the old Rover plant at Longbridge, with body panels and sub-assemblies to be provided (by rail) from the existing Rover body plant at Swindon (not far from Oxford) *and* from the Land Rover factory at Solihull, with manual gearboxes (of

The one millionth Mini in final preparation at the Oxford plant.

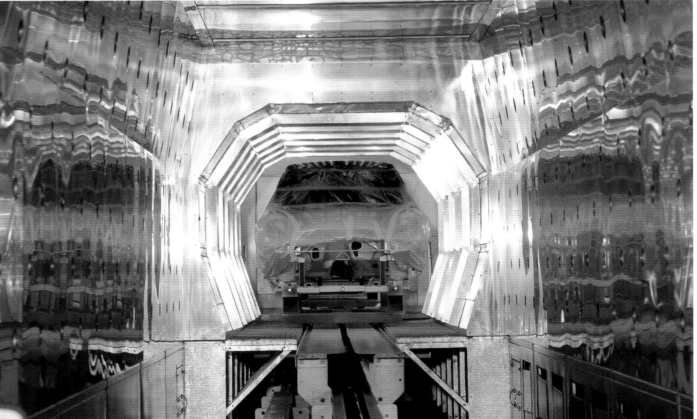

A new-generation MINI passes through an infra-red facility in the paint shop at BMW's Plant Oxford.

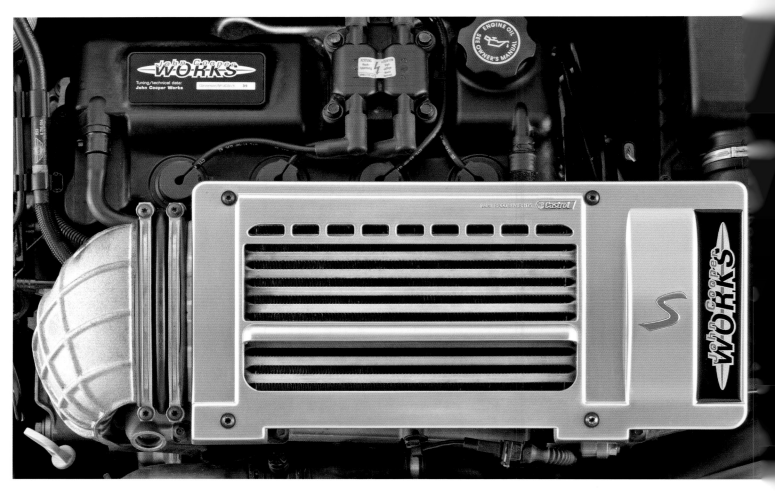

A skilled worker presses camshaft guides into the all-alloy block at the Ham's Hall engine plant.

ABOVE RIGHT
A Mini Cooper S engine tuned to the specification of Mike Cooper, son of Cooper cars founder, John Cooper.

modified Rover type) to be manufactured in another corner of Longbridge. After the "divorce," all that had to change—gradually at first, but completely within five or six years. As far as final assembly was concerned, the cataclysmic move from Longbridge to Oxford has already been described, but this, and later developments, all had to change to suit.

First of all, there was the question of body panel supply. Under BMW and Rover, the huge stampings/sub-assembly plant at Swindon (which employed up to 6,000 staff) had been used to supplying pressings to Longbridge and Land Rover at Solihull. Now it was faced with supplying pressings to Plant Oxford as well. Not only that, but an enormous multi-action press at Solihull was also due to supply massive pressings to Oxford too.

Complex? In the years that followed, it got more complex than ever. First of all, with Land Rover sold to Ford, this meant that Ford became a BMW supplier in a very big way, and when the (ex-BMW) Rover Group called in the liquidators in 2005, all the pressings business from Swindon to Longbridge came to an abrupt end.

By 2008, when Land Rover once again changed hands, but when there seemed no prospect of Longbridge being brought back to life by its new Chinese owners, BMW's MINI situation seemed to be more transparent than before. Pressings supply from Solihull had ended, the Swindon plant had become a dedicated MINI subsidiary (this was advertised, proudly, on the walls outside the plant), and Swindon's supply of pressings to

Land Rover was due to run out at the next model change. BMW's planners, and financial accountants, could finally heave a sigh of a relief.

The MINI engine business, complex at first, but simplified by 2008, finally made sense too. In the beginning, BMW had set up a joint project with Chrysler, whereby the same basic engine would be fitted to the new MINI, and to some Chrysler Corporation products. For fiscal reasons, it was decided to set up Tritec Motors Ltda, to build this engine at a new factory in Campo Largo, not far from Sao Paolo in Brazil—the arrangement being that engines for Oxford would be sent across the South and North Atlantic by the ship-load. (Diesel engines for the first-generation new MINI were eventually supplied by Toyota, and second-generation MINI diesels came from Peugeot in France.)

Functionally, the project worked well enough—until, that is, Chrysler let the side down by selling very few of their automobiles with this engine fitted. This meant that BMW had to take most of the output, and to bear most of the running expenses in Brazil. Accordingly, when the time came to develop a second-generation new MINI, BMW got together with PSA (Peugeot-Citroen) to design an all-new range of small gasoline engines. As already explained, these eventually went into production at Ham's Hall (for BMW), and in France (for Peugeot, Citroen *and* Ford models), and were soon recognized as a great success. Within months, incidentally, the latest MINI had been joined by the new Peugeot-sourced diesel engine too.

When the original new MINI was first engineered by Rover in the mid-1990s, BMW was reluctantly persuaded to approve the use of an existing front-wheel-drive Rover five-speed gearbox. At the design stage this made sense, for it was being manufactured at the Rover factory at Longbridge, only a step from where final assembly was due to take place. Then came the "divorce" of 2000, and regular supplies had to be trucked down the M40 motorway to Oxford. This difficult situation lasted only until the end of 2003. By that time a six-speed German Getrag box had been chosen for the MINI Cooper S, followed by a five-speed Getrag for lesser-powered MINIs. By then, incidentally, up to 5,000 MINIs were being produced at Oxford every week (the plant seemed to be run virtually on a round-the-clock basis to achieve this), and annual production was close to the 250,000-a-year mark. With new derivatives appearing all the time—the estate-like Clubman went on sale in 2007, and the four-wheel-drive SAV version was due in 2009—the gamble in relocating MINI to Oxford had certainly paid off.

MINI tailgates ready for painting at the Swindon plant.

A new MINI Clubman at the Oxford plant awaits the installation of its power train.

Rolls-Royce Phantom pictured against a backdrop of the Golden Gate Bridge, San Francisco.

Rolls-Royce—the legend goes German

Although this book is mainly concerned with BMW, it would be quite wrong to ignore Rolls-Royce, the legendary British brand that BMW finally came to control from 2003. But how did it happen? For a few years, between 1998 and 2003, this was a very complicated story.

The saga really began in 1931 when Rolls-Royce, still independent at that time, took over Bentley, rapidly integrated the two companies, and kept the two brands going after the Second World War. For fifty years after 1946 (when the first post-war Bentley and Rolls-Royce automobiles were launched), automobiles carrying the two famous badges were often clones

of each other. Separated from its aerospace parent company in the 1970s, Rolls-Royce then found it difficult to survive alone, and accepted a takeover bid from the Vickers Group in 1980. During the 1990s, Vickers commissioned the design of new Rolls-Royce and Bentley models, choosing to power them by BMW V12 and turbocharged V8 engines respectively. Their launch, in a much-modified Rolls-Royce factory at Crewe, in England, was due in 1998. Before then, however, Vickers (which had also absorbed Cosworth), decided to rid themselves of all its automotive connections, and the business was put up for sale. There followed a positively unseemly scrabble for ownership, with VW thinking they could acquire both brands, and BMW

only being interested in Rolls-Royce. The battle would also involve the Rolls-Royce aircraft engine concern (which held trade mark rights to the *automobile* company's badge), and BMW, who had aircraft engine links with Rolls-Royce.

This is a much-compressed version of how BMW then secured the Rolls-Royce brand. When VW paid top dollar (£479 million/$850 million) for the Rolls-Royce Motor Cars business in April 1998, it secured the rights to Bentley too. In the meantime Rolls-Royce Ltd, the entirely separate aerospace business, which still owned trade mark rights to the famous automobile brand, then promised it to BMW, though VW objected vigorously. BMW threatened to withdraw engine

supplies from current models if they persisted. After an unseemly squabble, which was not publicly settled until July 1998, VW bowed to the inevitable, and agreed to hand over the brand to BMW—but this was not to become effective until January 1, 2003. BMW, for its part, got on with the design of a new Rolls-Royce automobile, which would be launched after that date—and had to make a decision as to where to build it. Design work on the all-new automobile began in 1999, and final approval came from the directors a year later,

The automobile itself—mainly packed with existing or evolutionary BMW running gear, in a brand-new structure—came about in an altogether logical way, but the choice of

The state-of-the-art Goodwood buildings are typical of the style of a European car plant in the twenty-first century.

171

The lines of the Phantom could be said to be a fusion between traditional British Rolls-Royce styling and BMW's own design ethos.

BELOW
The Rolls-Royce assembly line at the Goodwood manufacturing plant.

factory took time. Because the structure was to be crafted from light-alloy, and produced at Dingolfing (where the aluminum-based Z8 sports car had also been made), the purely logical site for BMW-owned Rolls-Royce assembly was at Dingolfing, but top management decided not to do this. Perhaps more than any other automotive brand in the world the public perceived the Rolls-Royce as a purely British brand, which must remain British-built at all costs. Accordingly, BMW set about finding a factory in Britain to make the automobile. Because there was no question of building the new automobile at Crewe, which became a dedicated Bentley-own enterprise, a number of possible locations were investigated before a site at Goodwood in Sussex, close to the historic motor racing circuit, and in the Goodwood House estate itself (where the Festival of Speed is held every year), was chosen.

Designed by a British architect, and costing £65 million/$115 million to build and equip, Goodwood was in an area with no previous automobile-building expertise. However, because it was close to the sea near Chichester there was high-class boat building expertise in abundance, so the question of fitting out the bodies to the right standard was never in doubt. The factory itself was partly designed around a redundant quarry—because it was in such beautiful parkland, it had to be as unobtrusive as possible. In the single-story layout the floor was sunk about 5

The Rolls-Royce manufacturing plant and head office at Goodwood in England.

feet (1.5 meters) below the natural ground level, and the curved roof was grassed over to help it to blend into the countryside. A large artificial lake made it look cool, and there was a huge glass wall with automated sun shades that allowed visitors and customers to see automobiles being built.

The new model, to be named Phantom (thus reviving a famous badge of the past) was to be superlative in all respects and (as we now know) was merely the first of a family of new Rolls-Royces that BMW planned to put on sale. Because of this, BMW skimped nothing on the style, nor the engineering, nor the fit and finish of this colossal four-door machine. And colossal it certainly was—when the first road tests were published, they confirmed that this 5,500lb (2500kg) behemoth, which had a wheelbase of no less than 140.6 inches (3.5 meters), could reach 150mph/241kph—but at the cost of a fuel consumption of less than 15mpg (Imperial).

Although the abruptly squared off front-end style would always be controversial—the radiator grille and the headlamps were definitely and defiantly rectangular too—the Dingolfing-constructed four-door body shell was a technical masterpiece. Like the unlamented Z8, the new Phantom took shape around an aluminum "space frame," almost every other panel was pressed or die-cast aluminum too (front wings were in scrape-resistant sheet-molded composite). Rear doors were hinged at the rear, and automatically locked into place above 2.5mph/4kph (which is why BMW bridled at the oft-repeated, totally inaccurate, description of these as "suicide" doors). When completed, the monocoques were then to be transported, three at a time, to Goodwood for painting, and completion.

The running gear—453bhp/6.75-liter V12 engine, six-speed ZF automatic transmission, huge four-wheel disc brakes, and all-independent suspension by air springs—was developed from that of the latest 7-Series, but also featured colossal wheels (21in./52.5cm diameter was standard) and—a nice touch, this—the "RR" badges in the center of those wheels were free to spin, and weighted, so that when the automobile came to rest, they always settled in the letters-vertical position! With a sumptuous interior—leather, wood and thick pile carpet in abundance as expected—here was a hand-built automobile that was bound to sell in hundreds rather than in thousands, which is what it did. In 2004, the first full year of Goodwood's existence, a mere 700 automobiles were completed. That number increased substantially in the years that followed, but was always going to be dwarfed by the achievement of sites like Dingolfing and Munich. Before the end of the first decade, shortened-wheelbase two-door cabriolet and fixed-head coupe derivatives had also been launched, and a second range (dubbed a "baby Rolls-Royce" by the more excitable pundits) was also being developed.

Meanwhile, back at base...

While much of the glamor—of new products, new sales records, and new factories—was spread widely, BMW kept on pushing ahead with its own new models, and up-grading its existing facilities. The fact was, however, that spare capacity in most of its existing factories had virtually disappeared, and before long, one suspects, BMW would be faced with making strategic decisions such as—what existing plants could be expanded further, should a further brand-new plant be erected in Europe, and should the joint-enterprise plant at Shenyang (with Brilliance) be expanded to beyond its capacity of 30,000 automobiles a year?

In any case, new models had continued to pour out of BMW in recent years, and it is worth recalling what they were, and when they arrived: (continues on 189)

ABOVE RIGHT

Almost there—all the mechanical equipment on this BMW 3-Series seems to have been fitted, at Munich—but wheels, some trim material, and final checks all remain to be carried out.

RIGHT

Yet another 3-Series body shell, at the very beginning of the paint process—after which the shell will be taken to the assembly line for all the mechanical items to be fitted.

OPPOSITE

The fitting of the exhaust emission system on an M5 model at the Dingolfing Plant, Germany.

ABOVE
The paint of all modern BMWs was automatically applied by ultra-flexible robots, though these were kept strictly under human control.

TOP RIGHT
Once completed, every modern BMW was subjected to checks on the rolling road at the end of every assembly line, the demands on the car being checked by the driver.

BELOW RIGHT
Brakes OK? Controls OK? Transmission OK? Power output OK? All this, of course, was checked on the rolling road installation of every modern BMW factory.

The BMW 1-Series was launched in the mid-2000s, and instantly became BMW's best-selling "entry-level" model.

BELOW LEFT
A 1-series bodyshell is dipped in a bath of phosphate solution at the Regensburg plant.

BELOW
Why use human labor when a robot can do the job instead? This electronically controlled machine is installing seats into the 1-Series hatchback.

This body-in-white 1-Series hatchback is now ready to go through the anti-corrosion and paint process at Regensburg. Facilities like this were duplicated in several BMW plants across the world.

Every 5-Series is subject to functional checks, including brake tests, after it has been assembled at Dingolfing.

Ready to leave, for delivery to the customer, this 7-Series is approaching the end of the moving production line at Dingolfing.

Last-minute checks as a modern 7-Series prepares to leave the assembly lines at Dingolfing.

Apart from having its electrical systems checked out, this 7-Series is complete, at the ultra-modern Dingolfing factory.

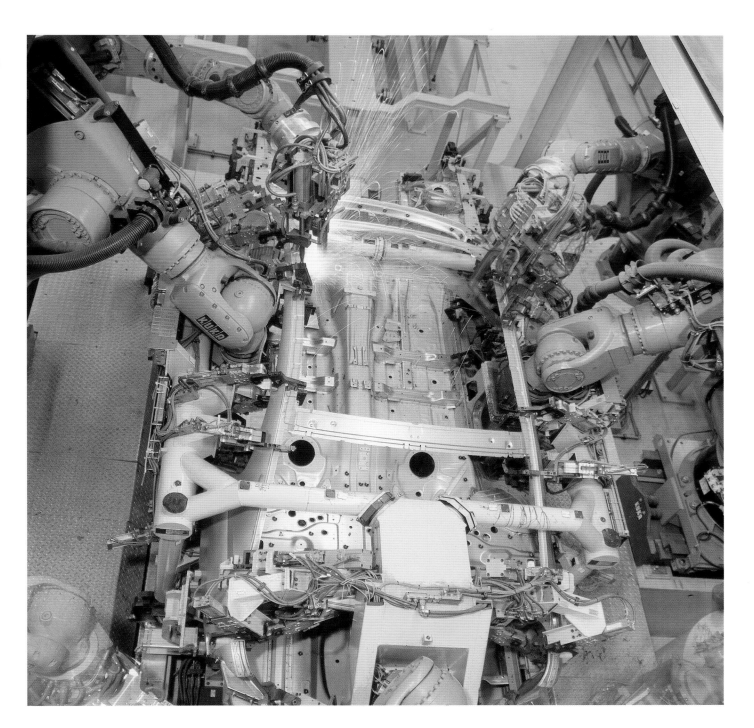

LEFT
Floor pan assembly under way at Dingolfing, with several high-tech robots, but not a single human being, in sight.

OPPOSITE TOP LEFT
Since its massive reconstruction in the 1970s, and subsequently, the Dingolfing plant has become the largest BMW car manufacturing plant of all. In modern times, it not only built 5-Series, 6-Series and 7-Series cars, but also constructed body structures for the Rolls-Royce Phantom model.

OPPOSITE BOTTOM LEFT
The miracles of automation! This robot is installing the entire fascia/air-conditioning and instrument panel assembly of a 3-Series, through the door aperture of the body shell, at the Leipzig factory.

OPPOSITE TOP RIGHT
Always a ticklish job—though aided by accurate alignment by the machinery, is the "body drop" (or "marriage" stage in BMW assembly, where the shell is gently lowered on to the already-assembled engine, running gear and suspension units.

OPPOSITE BOTTOM RIGHT
Once assembly has been completed, every BMW—this is a 3-Series—is subjected to rolling-road tests to see that it meets standards.

RIGHT
Inspection of newly pressed body panels is carried out by ultra-sensitive probes, aided by computers. This is the right rear quarter panel of a 7-Series, where the fuel filler recess is located.

FACING PAGE
To get the maximum output from factories such as Dingolfing, BMW arranged for huge body shell storage facilities at strategic points in the flow-line process. Priorities can therefore be changed at relatively short notice.

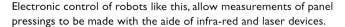

Electronic control of robots like this, allow measurements of panel pressings to be made with the aide of infra-red and laser devices.

TOP
Can this really be a car production factory, not a research laboratory ? In this area, ultra-sonic techniques are used to control the placing and intensity of welding spots.

ABOVE
Strong lights above the constantly moving assembly line at Dingolfing, mean that this BMW 7-Series will be carefully scrutinized before it leaves the factory.

FAR LEFT
Part way through the painting process, a 7-Series goes through the infra-red drying chamber.

LEFT
Seat assembly taking place—the frame being supported at the optimum height for the assembly worker.

OPPOSITE
The bestselling X3 is unique as it is produced in the award-winning plant of Magna Steyr in Graz, Austria which is not owned by BMW.

BELOW LEFT
A selection of high-grade leather being inspected, before seat assembly begins.

LEFT
The BMW 5-series reaches its 5-millionth car on 29 January, 2008.

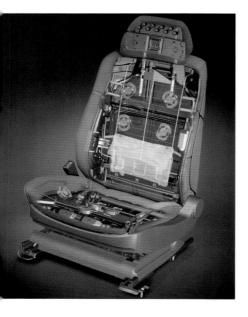

ABOVE
Not only is every aspect of a modern BMW seat adjustable—for rake, height, reach and the contour of the backrest—but there was active ventilation and, on some models, heating too.

ABOVE RIGHT
BMW adopted "doors-off" assembly methods some years ago, so that bulky components such as seats, and fascia/instrument panels, could be inserted with ease. Every assistance was given to the workforce to reduce the effort involved.

RIGHT
Swivel assembly—the cars being carried in massive cages—allows all BMW components to be fixed to the body shells at a height ideal for the worker responsible for that task.

Steering column, fascia, instrument and gearshift componentry all going into place on the final assembly line.

Assembly of the center console (including the I-Drive-Controller, and seat-adjustment controls, at the Dingolfing plant.

BMW
1-SERIES SEDANS, COUPES, CONVERTIBLES
Launched in 2005. Assembled at Regensburg and
Leipzig.
3-SERIES SEDANS, TOURERS, COUPES AND CONVERTIBLES
Launched in 2004. Assembled at Munich, Regensburg,
Leipzig, Rosslyn (South Africa), Shenyang (China)

5-SERIES SEDANS, TOURERS
Launched in 2003. Assembled at Dingolfing

6-SERIES COUPES, AND CABRIOLETS
Launched in 2003. Assembled at Dingolfing

7-SERIES SEDANS
Launched in 2001. Assembled at Dingolfing

X3 4x4 SAV (ESTATES)
Launched in 2003. Assembled at Magna-Steyr, Austria

X5 4x4 SAV (ESTATES)
New version launched in 2006. Assembled at
Spartanburg, USA

X6 4x4 "CROSS-OVER" COUPES
Launched in 2007. Assembled at Spartanburg, USA.

Z4 ROADSTERS
Launched in 2002. Assembled at Spartanburg, USA

MINI
Second-generation, launched in 2006. Assembled at
Oxford, England

ROLLS-ROYCE
Phantom, launched in 2003. Assembled at Goodwood,
England

In an atmosphere of unbroken confidence, there seemed to be no
limit to BMW's ambitions for the future, which meant that
watchers and industrial observers watched avidly to see how the
story would develop. One thing was certain—that everything we
knew about BMW in 2000 had been transformed by 2010, and
that knowledge would no doubt be outdated again soon. And
that, for a company whose first automobile had not been built
until 1929, and whose premises had been flattened by bombing
in 1945, was a remarkable achievement.

OPPOSITE
Because the BMW 6-Series of the
2000s had much in common with
the 7-Series sedan, it was
manufactured in the same plant,
at Dingolfing, north-east of
Munich.

ABOVE
The BMW X6 4x4 "cross-over"
coupe will be made at
Spartanburg in the USA.

INDEX

ACKNOWLEDGEMENTS

The Publishers would like to thank the following for their help in compiling this book.

Martin Harrison, BMW Group UK
Caroline Schulenburg, BMW Group Classic
Ruth Standfuss, BMW Group Archive
Matt Thornton, Rolls-Royce Motor Cars Ltd.
Dr. Florian Triebel, BMW Group Classic
Kristina Weber, BMW Group Archive
Chris Willows, BMW Group UK